and
Architects

The Anne Burnett Tandy Lectures in American Civilization

NUMBER TWO

PATRONS and ARCHITECTS:

JOHN COOLIDGE

Designing Art Museums in the Twentieth Century

AMON CARTER MUSEUM • FORT WORTH, TEXAS • 1989

Library of Congress Cataloging-in-Publication Data

Coolidge, John, 1913–
    Patrons and architects.
    (The Anne Burnett Tandy lectures in
American civilization ; no. 2)
    Includes index.
    1. Art museums—United States—History
—20th century. 2. Architects and patrons
—United States. I. Title. II. Series.
NA6695.c6 1989   727'.7'0904 88-82613
ISBN 0-88360-058-7

The Amon Carter Museum was established in 1961 under the will of Fort Worth publisher and philanthropist Amon G. Carter, Sr. (1879–1955). Initially comprised of Carter's collection of paintings and sculpture by Frederic Remington and Charles M. Russell, the Museum has since broadened the scope of its collection to include American paintings, prints, drawings, and sculpture of the nineteenth and early twentieth centuries, and American photography from its beginnings to the present day. Through its collections, special exhibitions, public programs, and publications, the Museum serves as a center for the study and appreciation of American art.

Contents

for
Richard Krautheimer

Acknowledgments

This book originated as a series of three Anne Burnett Tandy Lectures given in 1980 at the Amon Carter Museum, Fort Worth, Texas. I wish first to express my thanks to Mr. William Howze, Program Director, for his kindness both in inviting me and supporting my lectures. Mr. Ron Tyler, formerly Assistant Director for Collections and Programs at that Museum and presently Director of the Texas State Historical Association in Austin, was a model of patient understanding, and made many helpful suggestions in the rewriting of these lectures for publication. His assistant at the Museum, Mr. Ben Huseman, continued his many courtesies. To Matthew Abbate, the Museum's Publications Coordinator, I cannot adequately express my gratitude for his conscientious and sensitive editing of my manuscript and for carrying it through to publication.

For specific illustrations I am greatly indebted to the following present or former staff members of the institutions named: Ms. Helle Crenzien of Louisiana; Mr. Marshall Myers, Mr. Jules Prown, and Ms. Marilyn Hunt of the Yale Center for British Art; Ms. Ann Kraft of the Guggenheim Museum; Ms. Rosemarie Roth of the Artemis Verlag, Zurich; Mme. Evelyne Trehin of the Fondation Le Corbusier; Herr Reinhard Friedrich of Berlin; Mr. Richard Tooke of the Museum of Modern Art; Ms. Rita M. Cacas of the National Gallery of Art, Washington; Ms. Rosmarie Helsing of Zurich; Miss Rochelle Ziskin of Cambridge, Massachusetts; Mme. Françoise Marquet of the Centre Georges Pompidou and Mme. Catherine Lawless and M. Gérard Regnier of the Musée National d'Art Moderne, Paris; Ms. Shirley Hind and Mr. James Stirling of London; and Mr. Timothy Hursley of Little Rock, Arkansas.

This book would not have been possible without the advice and cooperation of the staff of all the museums discussed. The description of each museum has been shown in manuscript to a member of its staff, and although I alone am responsible for the opinions presented, they have contributed many corrections of fact, invaluable suggestions, and much practical help in providing or enabling me to find illustrations. I wish to express especial thanks to Mr. Rollin Hadley of the Isabella Stewart Gardner Museum, Mr. Philip Johnson, Mr. Knud W. Jensen of Louisiana, Mr. Duncan Robinson of the Yale Center for British Art, Mr. Thomas Messer of the Guggenheim Museum, Mr. Haruo Arikawa of the National Museum of Western Art in Tokyo, Mrs. Roberta Emerson and Mrs. Louise Polan of the Huntington Galleries, Mr. Alex E. Boothe, Jr., of Kenova, West Virginia, Dr. Lucius Grisebach of the National Gallery, Berlin, Mr. J. Carter Brown of the National Gallery of Art, Washington, M. Gérard Regnier of the Musée National d'Art Moderne and M. Christian Leprette, both of Paris, and Mr. James Stirling of London.

I am also deeply grateful to my colleagues at the Fogg Art Museum, Miss Agnes Mongan and Professors Seymour Slive and John M. Rosenfield, who have helped me in innumerable ways, with profoundly valuable advice over many years as well as with many valuable suggestions on specific points.

From the start my wife has been a constant support, as well as my most willing and severe critic. She has exercised exemplary patience at each delay in the preparation both of the original lectures and the manuscript of this book. Without her enduring encouragement and sensitive help at every stage, nothing would have been accomplished.

Introduction

I chose the architecture of art museums as the subject of these essays for three reasons. First, it is timely. There are few public activities that are increasing in their appeal so rapidly as museum-going. We have had to build, extend, and remodel, and we shall have to continue doing so. Almost all of our largest art museums—the National Gallery, the Metropolitan, Chicago, Boston, Los Angeles—have been involved in major building, or are about to become involved in such building. This is of course true of many museums of lesser size. During the 1980s four of the twelve museums discussed in this book—Louisiana, the National Museum of Western Art in Tokyo, the Museum of Modern Art in New York, and Beaubourg—have been significantly extended or rebuilt, and a fifth, the Guggenheim, plans an expansion.

Second, virtually every great twentieth-century architect has at least designed an art museum, and many have built one or more.[1] Moreover, the interest continues. In 1979 the Fogg Museum chose an architect for a new building. As a start they wrote to more than seventy architects, foreign and American, asking them to submit their work for consideration. Only one man said that he wasn't interested, despite the fact that this was to be a minimal job—60,000 square feet for an estimated $4.8 million ($80 a square foot). Philip Johnson has explained the enthusiasm behind this response. "Purely aesthetically speaking, the museum is an architect's dream. He has—as in a church—to make the visitor happy, to put him in a receptive frame of mind while he is undergoing an emotional experience. We architects welcome the challenge."[2] No other type of public, corporate, or community building has shown the same appeal to leading architects.

Third, the results have been variously disappointing. All the great twentieth-century architects have tried, and except when dealing with a single, narrowly limited problem, all have fallen short in one major respect or another. Some have produced buildings that were unforgettable sculpturally or spatially, but regrettable functionally. Other buildings worked well, but achieved little architectural individuality. Still others lacked consistency, being outstanding in one part, failures elsewhere. The all-but-universal public verdicts have been: "We would never try that again" or "Adequate, but not one of his best buildings."

In part, the problem lies with the institutions. Typically, the architect designing a new museum seeks to please three different groups of people: the patrons, or a single patron, that is to say a board of trustees or a single major donor; the professional staff, a body that traditionally sustains awkward relationships to the trustees; and finally the public, an amorphous group about which both trustees and staff sentimentalize, but about which usually little is known (and only rarely is there any serious desire to acquire hard information).[3]

And then there are the collections. Each of the three groups mentioned has a different attitude toward works of art. Small wonder there is confusion as to objectives, standards, and architecture.

Typically, the architect faces one of two situations. He is handed a detailed program by patron, trustees, or staff, and he creates a building exactly fulfilling that program. When conditions change, the exactly suitable becomes a white elephant. J. Paul Getty wanted an exact replica of a Pompeian villa, plus such modern conveniences as plumbing and parking. What can be done with it now? Alternatively, nobody knows what they want. Trustees or staff turn to the architect and say, "You must have thought about these things; you know about architecture; design us your ideal museum. Write your own program." Kevin Roche did just this at Oakland.

Those two situations suggest the approach followed here. The first chapter will deal with four museums that were created by or for single collectors; the second with four created in realization of their architect's vision; the last with some museums that were created by collaboration between the professional staff and the architect with the expressed intention of serving the public.

Museums are complex institutions. Plans, elevations, and sections are hard to come by. People relating to works of art are hard to photograph convincingly. So it seems best to discuss a relatively small number of examples and treat each in some detail. Emphasis will be on complete new buildings or virtually independent additions because these reveal the latest patterns of compromise, and therefore express present-day ideals most clearly. To put it negatively, there will be no discussion of re-modelings.

The Tandy Lectures are devoted to the study of American art and culture. Necessarily the principal emphasis will be on our art museums. But the problems are international, and ideas for solutions can be picked up over a wide range. A final limitation: I shall discuss only buildings I have seen. It is so hard to photograph art museums effectively that it is more than usually dangerous to evaluate buildings only from publications.

Within those considerations I shall be concerned with "quality," a seemingly obvious standard but one that, when applied to museums, can sometimes imply conflicting values. The Guggenheim is one of the great buildings of the twentieth century, but few would maintain that it is an ideal place to exhibit art. The Museum of Modern Art developed one of the great collections of this century, but as originally built it lacked space to display it adequately. Louisiana has neither of these distinctions but has proved exceptionally attractive to a wide range of visitors. Philip Johnson's small and little-known museum was chosen because it concerns itself with the proper way to exhibit sculpture, a major art whose particular architectural demands are usually overlooked. Similarly Louis Kahn's urbanistically distinguished Yale Center was selected principally because of its admirable and innovative display of the permanent collection of paintings.

Why do we build art museums? The generic answers are "We have this great collection" or "We are going to have a great collection" or "We want to have a great collection and the public should be able to enjoy it." So, to answer the question, you have to start with the story of Americans collecting works of art. Astonishingly, that story has not yet been adequately told. A useful point of departure is the guide to the United States that Baedeker published in 1893. Consider a few excerpts:

> The Metropolitan Museum of Art . . . is a somewhat unpretending building of red brick with granite facings. . . . In 1879, when moved into the present building, the collections were valued at $400,000; their present value is upwards of $7,000,000. Among the chief features of the museum is the Cesnola Collection of Cypriote antiquities. . . . These objects . . . were found by General Cesnola in 1865 and later years, while U.S. consul on the island of Cyprus. . . . General guide 10 c., special catalogues 10 c. each. Most of the objects are labelled.

In Boston, the Museum of Fine Arts is

> a somewhat restless piece of architecture, of red brick, with terracotta details. . . . The Ground Floor is mainly devoted to a large and excellent collection of Casts . . . surpassed in importance by those of Berlin and Strassburg only. [On the first floor,] the N. side contains the Collection of Paintings, most of which are on loan and frequently changed.

The Art Institute of Chicago possessed some very interesting and valuable collections, invisible, because at that moment the Art Institute was without a home.[4]

Today, not quite a century later, America occupies second place in almost every artistic field. The Egyptians say that we have the best Egyptian art outside Egypt. We have the best pre-Columbian art outside Latin America. We have the best Chinese paintings outside China, the best British art outside Great Britain, and so forth. Of course, there are exceptions—the Russians do better on Dutch seventeenth-century—but then consider our French nineteenth-century paintings. We have six of the seven great Seurats, and the only reason that the seventh is in France is that it was left to the Louvre by the New York collector John Quinn. The people largely responsible have been American private collectors. They have had the drive, the daring, the imagination, and the funds. Institutional collecting has been worthy but tame by comparison. Most people overlook the degree to which our great museum collections, notably those of our National Gallery, are made up of objects bequeathed by private individuals.

·I·
Sheltering
Private
Collections

Because of their overall contribution to national holdings of works of art, it is appropriate to begin with the museums created by great private collectors. They have certain traits in common. They represent the simplest kind of problem. One donor (rarely two) forms a collection, which because it reflects a single person is more coherent than the collection of a public museum. Such collectors know how they want their collection to be viewed, generally as a monument to themselves. The presentation of individual works of art and of the collection as a whole is designed to please this patron, and usually reflects a single point of view. He or she has the money to build and the sole right to choose the architect. Typically, these museums are more or less houses and often reflect the owner's image of himself as someone who lives right—flowers abound, there are provisions for occasional concerts, perhaps there is a small collection of books in handsome bindings. But there has been little attempt to analyze, much less cater to the varying interests of the different publics who might visit the museum. Basically, there are not many ways to admire a monument. Initially at least, there were likely to be few provisions for temporary exhibitions, for conservation laboratories, or for museum education.

The Gardner Museum

"Fenway Court," as it was originally called, is the oldest and most personal of the major private art museums in America. It was the creation of Isabella Stewart Gardner. Born in New York in 1840, she married John Lowell ("Jack") Gardner of Boston in 1860 and two years later moved into the conventional brownstone house her father had built for her on Beacon Street, the most fashionable street in that city.[1] Both families were wealthy and her husband became a successful businessman.

Intelligent, vital, charming, warm-hearted, happily married, rich, she loved her own family, loved and was deeply loved by the Gardners. She must have seemed endowed with every blessing; what followed was an extraordinary sequence of personal tragedies.[2] She was prostrated by the death of her son in 1865 at the age of two and it was three and a half years before she fully recovered. Recover she did, and by exceptional positive activity rose above every later personal disaster and disappointment, passionately felt though each one was.

In the end, hers was a multiple achievement. "Judging precisely the degree to which indiscretion might be carried, she excelled in that provocative but never too flagrant behavior which established her as the town's most alluring personality and supreme hostess."[3] She became a devoted patron of contemporary artists, musicians especially. Always her patronage was of individuals; she was "perhaps the most personally involved benefactress of her day."[4] She recurrently provided the warmest of welcomes and friendship to men such as John Singer Sargent, Henry James, and Bernard Berenson, distinguished American intellectuals who had chosen to live abroad. Ultimately she became a connoisseur of literature and a collector of most types of the visual arts. She bought rare books, fine bindings, old masters, and the paintings of advanced artists of her own generation such as Degas and Manet. She accepted as a gift, and proudly displayed, a painting by Henri Matisse, before any museum in America had done so. An early work by Schoenberg was performed in at least one of the concerts she presented. It was as a background for this depth of affection and wealth of activity that she conceived Fenway Court.[5]

In 1873 she bought her first significant works of art, a painting by Jacque as well as a drawing (supposedly) by Rembrandt, and in 1879 eleven pieces of fifteenth-century stained glass. Mr. Gardner's father died that same year, and thereafter they were able to buy more and better works of art, for example in 1880 paintings by William Morris Hunt and Corot, a Vittoria bronze door knocker, and six tapestries.

At this time Mr. Gardner inherited Green Hill, his parents' suburban house in Brookline. In addition they had a summer house in Beverly, Massachusetts, so, normally, Beacon Street was occupied only during the winter months.

The Gardners were enthusiastic

1. *Isabella Stewart Gardner Museum, Boston, completed 1903. Exterior from the Fenway; dull yellow brick with red tile roof.*

travelers, going around the world in 1883 and thereafter spending several months in Europe every other year. They bought works of art everywhere they went as well as in the United States, now Renaissance sculpture, now a madonna from Zurbarán's studio, now Oriental or European textiles. But at first there was no consistent pattern of acquisition.

The death of Mrs. Gardner's father in 1891 introduced a great change. She inherited two and three-quarter million dollars and soon resolved to collect important old masters. In pursuing them she sought the help of several younger men, Ralph Curtis, John Singer Sargent, Joseph Lindon Smith, Richard Norton, and especially Bernard Berenson.

In an initial splurge between May and December 1892 she bought a Pesellino, a Cranach, a Suttermans, and a Vermeer, as well as a Rosetti, a Whistler, five fifteenth-century tapestries, a Gothic relief of St. George, and seven polychromed armchairs that were said to have belonged to Pope Paul V. Toward the end of her life, Paul Clemen, the eminent professor of art history at Bonn, could write: "Certainly you have now the best private collection in the world—not the largest, but the noblest. . . . The Wallace Collection suffocates now under the pictures and art objects. . . . In your house one walks quickly through the centuries and through the leading art countries and has always again quite a harmonious and round impression."[6]

What were Mrs. Gardner's intentions? As a girl she had visited the Poldi-Pezzoli collection in Milan and told a companion: "If I ever have any money of my own, I am going to build a palace and fill it with beautiful things."[7] But the British inspired the way she used her palace. Baedeker put it

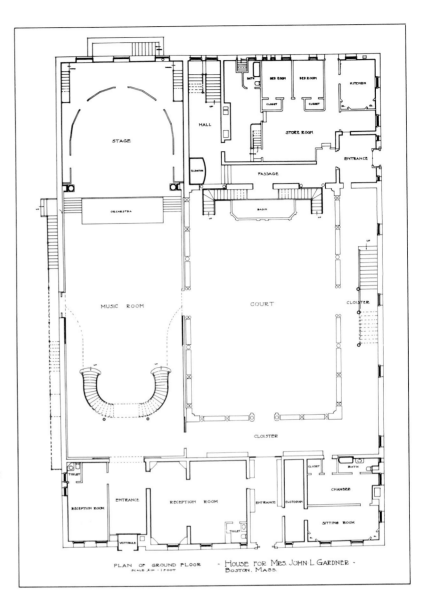

2. *Gardner Museum. Ground floor as originally planned. The entrance to the Music Room was on the left. Note that there was no cloister between the Music Room and the court. The usual entrance to the building was center right with a small apartment beyond.*

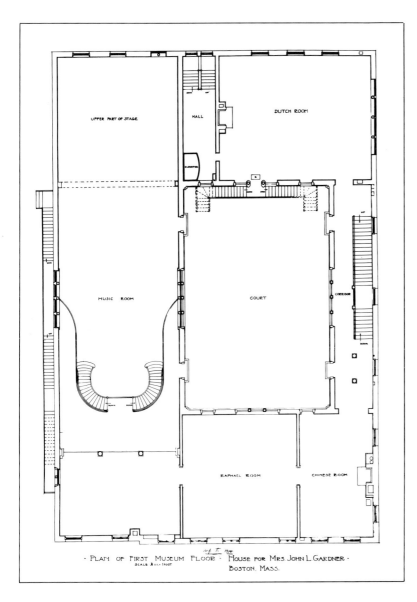

3. *Gardner Museum. Second floor as originally planned. The function of the lower left corner room is unclear; perhaps it served as a balcony during concerts.*

succinctly. "The English aristocracy . . . reside in the country during the greater part of the year; but it is usual for the principal families to have a mansion in London, which they occupy during the season, or at other times when required. . . . Many of these are worth visiting, not only on account of the sumptuous manner in which they are fitted up, but also for the sake of the treasures of art which they contain. . . . The residence of the Duke of Sutherland is perhaps the finest private mansion in London, and contains a good collection of paintings, which is shown to the public on certain fixed days in spring and summer. Application for admission should be made to the Duke's secretary."[8]

By the mid-nineties, the Gardners had decided to build themselves such an establishment. In 1896 Mrs. Gardner met the complaisant eclectic architect Willard T. Sears as both were going to a funeral. She told him they proposed to tear down their establishment on Beacon Street and asked him to prepare plans for a five-story replacement on the same site. Although there was to be a court in the middle, necessarily this would be a row house.

Gradually Mr. Gardner became convinced that the Beacon Street property was too small, even with the potential purchase of adjacent houses. He expressed a preference for an open site on the as-yet-undeveloped Fenway. But he died unexpectedly in early December 1898.

On December 30 Sears brought the drawings for the Beacon Street museum to Mrs. Gardner, only to learn that she had bought a lot 100 feet by 150 feet on the Fenway. As the architect noted in his diary: "She wanted me to make new drawings and to include a small theater within the museum; the museum was to be one story less

4. *Gardner Museum. The original Music Room. Note the plaster relief at the head of the stairs; the Gardners had several plaster replicas of Florentine Renaissance reliefs in their Beacon Street house. The plaster figures around the walls recall the plaster replicas of famous classical statues still standing in their niches above the hoi poloi inside McKim, Mead & White's Boston Symphony Hall (recently completed when Fenway Court was built). The mirror on the left could slide into the wall, providing direct access to the court.*

in height than the one drawn for her at 152 Beacon Street. She wanted the drawings made as soon as possible."⁹

How soon was possible? We know only that by March 21 certain drawings were ready. Pile driving began in June. In August Mrs. Gardner received in Venice plans and some elevations of the building, substantially as it was ultimately erected (fig. 2).

Mrs. Gardner could stubbornly refuse to reconsider a decision already made. One of the advantages of the Fenway was the fact that the museum would be freestanding and could receive light from four sides. Mrs. Gardner retained all the essentials of the original plans. Though surrounded by gardens and parks, Fenway Court is basically a row house; the visitor naturally looks inward toward the court.

On the exterior Fenway Court is a four-story rectangular block, plain as a gymnasium (fig. 1). There is a two-story wing along all the left side. Originally, most of this was devoted to Sears' "theater," in fact a two-story music room for the concerts Mrs. Gardner enjoyed giving (figs. 2, 3, 4). The Music Room had its own entrance near the left-hand corner of the building. This led into a narrow passage flanked by lounges where music-lovers left their coats. In these modest bright rooms were Oriental objects and pleasant pictures by such familiar contemporary artists as Sargent, Whistler, Rosetti, and Diaz. Beyond the doorway to the Music Room was a horseshoe stairway. This the concertgoers climbed, greeting Mrs. Gardner where she stood alone in the center and descending to take their seats.

Fenway Court was designed for Mrs. Gardner's guests. But, beginning February 23, 1903, two hundred members of the public could look around on very occasional

"fixed days." For each of these Herrick's Agency sold tickets at a dollar apiece. This procedure was meant to qualify Fenway Court as an art museum and eventually justified exemption from real estate taxes. In addition, properly introduced visitors who applied by letter were allowed to investigate on their own.

Except for concerts and other special occasions, visitors used a doorway in the middle of the facade. This led into the main part of the house with its central court, a jungle of palms, flowers, and genuine classical statues around an ancient mosaic (fig. 5). Aside from the court and the concert hall the rooms on the ground floor were utilitarian, including a tiny apartment at the right front corner (fig. 2). Perhaps intended for a concierge, it was in fact occasionally lent to young artists. The top floor was Mrs. Gardner's apartment. Between were two floors of galleries, in each case a single large one at the back and three (more or less) at the front (figs. 3, 9, 10). A narrow stair hall along the west side of the court bound all together. A single artist or the works of one school gave each gallery a name, though in every case the content was somewhat mixed.

Mrs. Gardner was sixty-three when the museum opened and probably realized that she would not long wish to continue giving concerts and plays on a scale that required so ambitious a music hall. By 1908 architectural plans for a remodeling were complete.

Work began in February 1914. The great Music Room was divided in two horizontally by a floor at the level of its gallery. The space below was split into three parallel corridors, one becoming the eastern cloister walk of the court (fig. 6). The entire upper space of the auditorium—the void over orchestra, stage, green rooms—was

opened up into a vast tapestry room (fig. 7). Although it is actually sixteen feet high and has many windows, because of its forty-foot breadth and one hundred and ten feet of length the effect is curiously subterranean, though splendid, anticipatory, awesome.

Both front corner rooms were changed. Over the Music Room entrance was now yet another corridor, providing study storage for drawings and family portraits and appropriately named the Short Gallery. Beyond this the Little Salon is hung with tapestries and crowded with attractive personal gifts. At the opposite front corner there were no architectural changes, but what had been a gallery of Chinese art was now hung with early Italian paintings of exceptional quality.

Who was responsible for the architecture of Fenway Court? Morris Carter, whom Mrs. Gardner designated the first curator, declared: "Mr. Willard T. Sears . . . was engaged to submit plans; the drawings were made by Mr. Edward Nichols, but the design was entirely Mrs. Gardner's."¹⁰ One can believe she was responsible for the concept of a central court, a scheme she must have known well from Florentine palaces. It was the adaptation of this to a row house that produced the curiously narrow side wings in Fenway Court (fig. 8). After the decision was made to build a museum, first the Gardners together, later Mrs. Gardner alone passionately bought columns, capitals, architectural reliefs, and other decorative sculpture that play such a prominent part in the effect of the museum (fig. 5). Well known, too, is the intensity with which she involved herself in the process of building. She persuaded the dealer Bardini to let her have the formula for the blue paint she used in the corridors; she showed the workmen how she wanted the pink

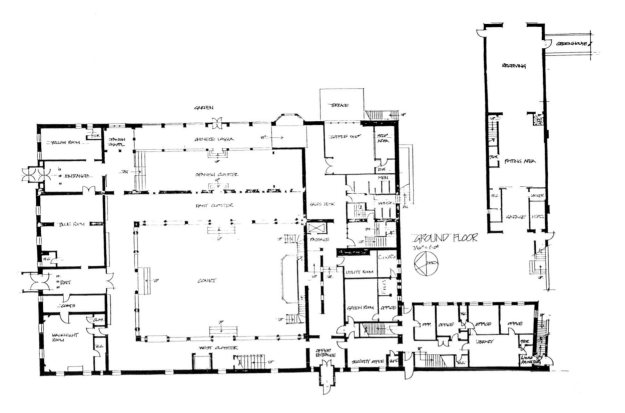

5. *Gardner Museum. The court-yard in 1915. The shrubbery had grown luxuriously. The flowers came from Mrs. Gardner's greenhouses in Brookline. Access to the stairs must have been along the sides of the court. The sculpture at the ground-floor level, like the mosaic, is from classical antiquity. Some capitals are genuine, others imitations. The arches, third floor center and extreme right and left, are originals from the Ca d'Oro in Venice, which had recently been restored; the reliefs are medieval and Renaissance. Most of the remaining decoration is imitation Venetian Gothic.*

6. *Gardner Museum. Plan of the ground floor as remodeled in 1914 and later. On this floor the Music Room was replaced by three parallel cloisters and the Spanish Chapel, a very private shrine in memory of Mrs. Gardner's son. The trustees added a wing and eventually trans-formed the entire rear portion of this floor into a small restaurant and of-fices for the Museum staff.*

paint applied to the court walls by splashing some of it on herself; she turned up daily as building proceeded.

To her lack of interest in effective planning one must attribute such peculiarities as the awkward passage from the Tapestry Room to the Dutch Room or the three parallel corridors on the east side of the ground floor (fig. 6). In fact she had little concern with conventional architectural values. The exterior of Fenway Court is boring (fig. 1), the interior a complex succession of independent rooms. The visitor rarely senses an evolving progression; it is the drama of contrast that leads him from one space to the next.

Fenway Court was conceived as a positive critique of contemporary museums. Of the Louvre Mrs. Gardner wrote: "I feel about it and many museums as I did about the Prado—if I could only take hold! Some things are so wonderful—and yet so badly presented—

7. *Gardner Museum. The Tapestry Room. This replaced the upper part of the Music Room; it has been used for concerts ever since. On this side of the fireplace are a table and chairs that Mrs. Gardner used for small but formal dinners. In 1916 or thereabouts she had considered the acquisition of a Spanish primitive but had not made up her mind. Meanwhile it was purchased by Paul Sachs, who had just moved to Cambridge from New York. Shortly Mrs. Gardner gave a highly select dinner party in his honor. Toward the close of the meal she remarked quietly: "Mr. Sachs, I understand you have just bought a Spanish primitive. Turn around. Don't you agree your painting would go very well over the fireplace?" Then she laid her right hand on the table and continued: "You know, this hand could hold a stiletto. If you tell me what you paid for your painting I will send you my check in the morning." Today it hangs over the fireplace and does look very well. (Told to me by Mr. Sachs.)*

8. *Gardner Museum. The Long Gallery, third floor left side. In plan this room nearly duplicates the stair hall across the court, thus connecting the sets of rectangular galleries front and back. This was essential to the row house concept carried over from the proposed remodeling of the Gardners' Beacon Street house.*

9. *Gardner Museum. The Dutch Room, second floor rear right. This contained the finest non-Italian paintings and was perhaps the most grandly hung of all the galleries. It became Mrs. Gardner's formal living room, visitors entering from the courtyard steps. It was used for the vernissage at the opening of the museum. In surprising ways Mrs. Gardner pinched her pennies. Edith Wharton was brought to that occasion by James Hazen Hyde and remarked of the conspicuously inadequate victuals: "Comme une gare de province." When it came time to depart she expressed her gratitude to Mrs. Gardner, who replied: "I am glad you enjoyed riding on my railroad, because I don't think you will have another chance." (Told to me, late in his life, by Mr. Hyde.)*

and such a lot of not good. Poor Museums! Strength of mind they do need—and taste." [11] Of the strength of Mrs. Gardner's mind there has never been any question. In her own taste she came to have complete confidence. But her objections to conventional museums largely concerned the way they displayed works of art.

Except for the Tapestry Room, Fenway Court contains only two significant kinds of space: tunnels and near-cubes (figs. 8, 9). Tunnels may have crowded walls, but everything is subordinated to a terminal accent, be it the bright light of the court viewed from the central entrance or the gorgeous stained-glass window terminating the Long Gallery. Cubes are often entered at one corner. This presents two walls in diagonal perspective, heightening the awareness of the rectangularity, but also maximizing the number of paintings that the viewer sees at first glance (fig. 9).

Within the individual cubes, Mrs. Gardner was concerned with three things: the initial impact on the visitor when entering, the provision of as much daylight on the principal paintings as she thought desirable, and the path of the visitor through the room. There is little concern for the viewer's relation to the daylight. Frequently he is all but blinded by the windows he faces. Equally there is no consideration of how the windows relate to the space of the room. Such is the arrangement of partitions that the windows are rarely symmetrically arranged on the main walls of the major rooms.

Mrs. Gardner's basic preference was for symmetrical hanging, but the hanging of paintings might be determined by quite other considerations, similarity of subject and treatment, for example. At one time, her Pollaiuolo profile portrait, Manet's portrait of his mother, and Degas' *Madame Gaujelin* all hung together in the Long Gallery because all the figures are middle-aged women dressed in black. The Uccello profile portrait is still close by the "Della Robbia bust of Marietta Strozzi"; both subjects are young. Another consideration was historical appropriateness. Thus Cellini's bust is placed beside what Mrs. Gardner bought as a portrait of Michelangelo (fig. 11). A favorite device was to place major paintings beside a window and at right angles to it—thus the Giotto, the Masaccio, the Fra Angelico, the "Giorgione," the two Raphaels, the Titian, Rembrandt's Obelisk, and the Vermeer. In terms of lighting the presentation, as with the Raphaels, can be admirable (fig. 10).

By contrast, Mrs. Gardner had little feeling for the display of sculpture. The principal ancient pieces are scattered about the courtyard, which in her day came to be far more of a jungle than it is now (fig. 5). None look well, and some are quite scandalously misplaced. For example there is a Severan sarcophagus, "one of the most elegant examples of Roman imperial mannerist elongation to have survived to Renaissance and later times." [12] Only one of its four carved sides can be seen properly. Her powerful bronze bust by Cellini is the least noticed of the great works of art in the collection (fig. 11). It rarely receives sufficient light and suffers from being against a dark background. Indeed, the only object displayed so that its sculptural quality tells is Mrs. Gardner's sedan chair.

This limitation is responsible for the greatest weakness of the collection, the furniture (figs. 9, 10, 11). Indifferent in quality, it is so unimaginatively placed that one always suspects it has been temporarily moved to wherever it is while workmen repair the patch of floor where it properly belongs.

By contrast, the collection of textiles is extraordinary. The most distinctive aspect of Fenway Court is the presentation of paintings and textiles together. Thus a wall of disparate small paintings will be drawn together by hanging a splendid cope below them. A fireplace will be framed by velvet curtains in such a way that on entering the room the visitor sees two Raphaels brilliantly illuminated but does not see the window that provides the illumination (fig. 10).

After the museum was opened in 1903, new acquisitions were sometimes stored wherever space was available, and later moved into a prominent position when a new gallery was arranged. On other occasions a new work might be simply inserted into a virtually complete room, as the Bellini *Madonna and Child,* acquired in 1921, was placed on a table in one corner of the Raphael Room.

As a result of this way of proceeding, Fenway Court cannot be thought of as complete. The Tapestry Room is unified (fig. 7), but the Early Italian Room is a succes-

10. *Gardner Museum. The Raphael Room, second floor front center. On the writing table, left corner, is Raphael's Pieta, above it an early copy of a portrait by him.*

11. *Gardner Museum. The Titian Room, third floor front center. On the left is his Rape of Europa; on a stand to the right Cellini's portrait bust of Bindo Altoviti. Mrs. Gardner's greatest painting and greatest sculpture balance one another. The bust is harder to see than the illustration suggests, however, because the color of the bronze does not stand out against the dark fabric covering the walls.*

sion of chronologically related masterpieces rather than a coherent display. And the Gothic Room is anticlimactic. More could have been done, but not much more by a woman in her eighties.

Fenway Court has exerted a double influence. As an architectural type—a block containing a courtyard—it inspired a number of distinguished smaller museums built in the following decades, notably the Walters Art Gallery, the Worcester Art Museum, and the Fogg Art Museum. As a genus, Mrs. Gardner's personal museum has many followers, the Frick, the Johnson collection, the Walters, the Phillips, the Crocker, the Norton Simon, and the Getty. It is curious that such institutions occur along both Atlantic and Pacific coasts, but not in the center of the country. The solitary exception is the Taft Museum in Cincinnati. Otherwise when middle-westerners had ambitions to create their own museums, they emigrated, taking their collections with them; Freer from Detroit to Washington, Frick and Mellon from Pittsburgh to New York and Washington respectively, Avery Brundage from Chicago to San Francisco.

It is a tribute to the private collecting of art in the twentieth century that the laudatory statements quoted earlier are no longer even remotely true. Considering only America, among private collections that have become museums the Gardner is less remarkable than the Walters; as a group of pictures it is less distinguished than the Frick. But the total experience it offers is certainly the richest. It is a monument to a way of life, not to the greedy or chilly escape from the collector's primary work in the world of big business. The fact that this way of life has disappeared, that public opinion would hardly tolerate its revival, adds to rather than detracts from the impact Fen-

way Court makes as a period piece. It is an entirety reflecting the entirety of Mrs. Gardner. To paraphrase Henry James: It is in the presence of the wonderfully gathered and splendidly lodged Gardner collection that one feels the fine old disinterested tradition of Boston least broken.[13]

Philip Johnson's Sculpture Gallery

It would be hard to think of two collectors of the art of their times more different than Mrs. Gardner and Philip Johnson, or of museums more diverse than those that these two collectors evolved for themselves. Johnson was born in Cleveland in 1906 and grew up there. In the middle 1920s he was one of an exceptional group of young people associated with Harvard who were passionately interested in the arts of the twentieth century. Since that time, each of them has made a remarkable contribution to the understanding and support of those arts, as well as the arts of other periods.[14]

Some years after graduating in 1927 Johnson became the first director of the Department of Architecture at the recently founded Museum of Modern Art in New York. Possibly the best-remembered achievement during his tenure of that post was the exhibition "Modern Architecture." This, with its catalogue and an accompanying book entitled *The International Style*, were executed with strong support from the director of the museum, Alfred Barr, and in collaboration with Henry-Russell Hitchcock, Jr.

Later, Johnson returned to Harvard and was granted a graduate degree in architecture in 1943. He established his practice in New York and came to be considered one of the most brilliant designers of his generation and one of the most successful practitioners of his art. All the while Johnson has collected contemporary painting and sculpture.

Johnson bought property in New Canaan, Connecticut, where in 1949 he built himself a small house with walls of clear glass. In subsequent years he added a windowless guest house, a garden pavilion, an underground storage and study suite for his collection of paintings, and in 1970 a gallery for his collection of sculpture.

At first view, the sculpture gallery appears to be a building of exceptional simplicity: an oddly shaped barn near the top of an open hillside (fig. 12). The roofs are blue-gray sloping skylights; the walls are painted brick, and so startlingly white they recall a Federalist church. Entering, you find yourself at the top corner of a surprisingly large white-walled room (figs. 13, 14). Above you five thousand square feet of bright ceiling rise in two simple slopes to an unbroken eighty-four-foot ridge pole. The glass of the ceiling is supported by aluminum tubes, closely spaced, like two-by-fours. Each carries on its under side a continuous cathode light. Thus the walls are patterned in patches by light bands coming from the glass and duller ones from the shadows of the beams. The effect is far gentler than any photograph suggests. The strange illumination is so pervasive that you are not conscious of zebra-striped surfaces, but rather you sense a total atmosphere gently vibrating.

Below you drops a deep well. Successive short flights of curbed stairs amble their spiral way around

12. *Philip Johnson Sculpture Gallery, New Canaan, Connecticut, 1970. Exterior.*

13. *Johnson Sculpture Gallery. Plan. The center of the building is a pentagonal court cut deeply into the hill, around which are four niche-like rooms. Beneath three of the niches are storage rooms accessible from the center.*

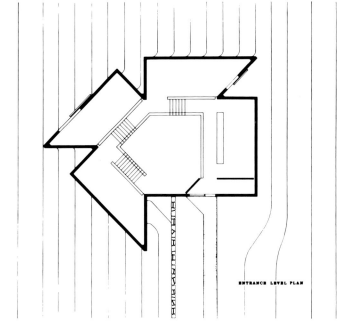

ENTRANCE LEVEL PLAN

14. *Johnson Sculpture Gallery. Interior facing the third niche. The entrance to this is through the rectangular opening under the bridge.*

15. *Johnson Sculpture Gallery. Sculpture by Donald Judd.*

it. They, like the floor at the bottom, are plum-colored. Alcoves, separated by prowlike partitions, open out intermittently (fig. 15). Here and there splendid sculptures are placed with apparent casualness, freestanding or against the walls (figs. 13, 14). One alcove may be dominated by a large composition in several media, another by elegantly wrought fluorescent tubes, glowing simply and powerfully in the palpitating atmosphere. Only one sculpture was commissioned for the building, a vertical succession of squares by Donald Judd. This has been moved to a different location, and, flatteringly, is now at least as effective as it was originally. Across the space the architect-host, until recently, might have sat comfortably in a Thonet chair awaiting your arrival.[15]

According to Johnson, as reported in an excellent article by John Morris Dixon, two considerations controlled the design of the building. For the first, "'Outdoor lighting is ideal for sculpture,' . . . and he has obtained a lighting effect which he calls 'reinforced outdoors' by using mirrored glass that transmits 14 percent of sunlight, then diffusing the light from the white walls and softening the shadows with lighting tubes attached to the rafters. ('When the sun is shining in, I always turn on the lights.')" For the second, "'The trouble with most sculpture gardens . . . is that you always see one work behind another. Here, each object is in its own niche.'"[16]

For all its exotic beauty, the sculpture museum is complete, behind the scenes. Johnson is most generous in lending the works of art he owns. This happens so frequently that he is continually replacing one sculpture by another. So he has provided ample storage space on the bottom floor.

First impressions and later recollections are vivid but imprecise. Those whose curiosity leads them further begin to discover that this is one of the most artfully intricate of twentieth-century buildings; so intricate that only careful study of its plans and elevations and sections yields clues to its recondite geometry. On a more immediate level there is the color contrast between the building and the works of art it contains and the opposition between the architecture as sculptured void and the statues as carved or molded solids. Three of the alcoves are identical in plan and area but differ markedly in height, in the way you approach them, and in the relation of their walls to the strongly beamed roof. Each is entered by a ninety-degree turn from the stairway, at the same corner of the alcove, but in one case this involves an immediate U-turn, in another you continue the direction of the stairway, in the third you cross the central floor space and go under a bridge. In a building devoid of decoration, these are telling differences. Johnson's extreme sensitivity to them is responsible for the subtle effectiveness with which he places and replaces individual pieces of sculpture.

It is stimulating to wonder how well traditional sculpture would fare in this environment. Rodin splendidly, for sure; but a gorgeously polychromed late-Gothic Madonna? A damaged Greek torso? But Johnson, expert at the design of small museums, could, one is confident, find a suitable solution for these and other ante-modern masterpieces as he did for Mayan artifacts at Dumbarton Oaks.

It is hard to think of another personal, secular building that parallels this museum in its elegance, its telling complexity, its individual flavor. The closest parallel may be a rococo masterpiece, the Amalienburg, that mid-eighteenth-century royal enjoyment house near the Nymphenburg palace in the woods outside Munich. Johnson knows Germany and German architecture well.

Louisiana

An interesting European counterpart to Philip Johnson's private museum is Louisiana, a museum of modern art eighteen miles north of Copenhagen created by Knud W. Jensen, a Danish businessman.[17] Jensen's father was a wholesale exporter who collected books. The younger Jensen wished to become an art historian but felt obliged to join the family business, which he managed with outstanding success until he sold it in the early 1950s. He then established the Louisiana Foundation and turned over to it much of the proceeds of the sale.

From his youth he was deeply interested in art, especially contemporary Danish work and those who created it. Thus, in order to support Danish writers, he became the principal stockholder of the Gylendel Press. While still in high school he started collecting the visual arts with the purchase of a drawing by Munch, and by the fifties he had more than a hundred paintings by living Danish artists as well as a notable collection of contemporary decorative art. His particular concern was with works he found characteristically Danish. Meanwhile he was evolving the philosophy that would shape the new museum he envisioned, a museum adapted to the social-democratic, prosperous, highly taxed, moderate, and motorized Scandinavia of our times.

His point of departure was the desirable relation of the individual to works of art. "One of the most prominent features—and problems—of the epoch we are moving into is *leisure*. We have hardly attained it before powerful forces are fighting to seize control of it: the entertainment industry and consumer mentality . . . which is precisely what we want to combat by demanding active interest

and a personal attitude and relation to the material we display."

Art makes a stronger impression when one's mind is purged by contact with the beauty of nature, and one meets it with renewed sensibility in something of that holiday mood where everything becomes new and fresh again. . . . Architecture, landscape gardening, sculpture, painting and the crafts are all expressions of the period we are living in, and ought—as far as may be—to be experienced together.

Pictorial art will always be of first importance at Louisiana, but we believe that the museum also has a part to play both together with and apart from the pictorial arts. During the past years music has been played, films shown and theater productions performed. There have also been panel discussions, happenings, and seminars. . . . The programs for film, concert and theater areas are planned as far as possible to correspond to the 8 to 10 exhibitions which are shown each year.[18]

Complementary to this concern with the public is Jensen's conviction that "in a period in which art has become more intellectual than formerly . . . it is important that the artist should meet his public, explain his work, and be prepared to discuss it."[19] Schoenberg and Stockhausen have conducted their own works in Louisiana's concert hall. Henry Moore was a frequent visitor and helped install the three of his sculptures that are part of the permanent collection. There is, on the grounds, a studio for visiting artists.

These convictions provide the basis for Louisiana. One fundamental change has taken place since Jensen conceived the institu-

tion. While the original idea was to present Danish art, design, and architecture, about 1966 "it became apparent that there was a need within Denmark for information about important trends in modern art outside the country." So now Louisiana's task is to exhibit twentieth-century art and exotic art of special appeal to contemporary artists (gold from Peru, Chinese peasant paintings), "as well as to build up a collection of works created after 1950." "We have no ambition to map out the complete historical development. The art of the last two decades is too pluralistic for this, and the space and funds at our disposal are far too limited. For many reasons we prefer to exhibit the work of relatively few artists—and preferably more than one piece by each. . . . The strongest focal point at Louisiana is without doubt the fourteen works by Giacometti."[20]

The change in artistic objective involved spending much more money on acquisitions. Since there was no corresponding increase in its own resources and no tax funds were available for this purpose, the museum turned to private individuals and foundations. Such was its success that a third of the interna-

16. *Louisiana Museum, Humlebaek, Denmark, established 1955. The original villa, c. 1850.*

17. *Louisiana. Site plan, showing the original building and five additions from 1958 to 1982, architects Jørgen Bo and Vilhelm Wohlert. Much sculpture is exhibited out of doors, large pieces (Moore and Calder) silhouetted against the ocean, smaller pieces (Ernst) set out on the grass and framed by trees.*

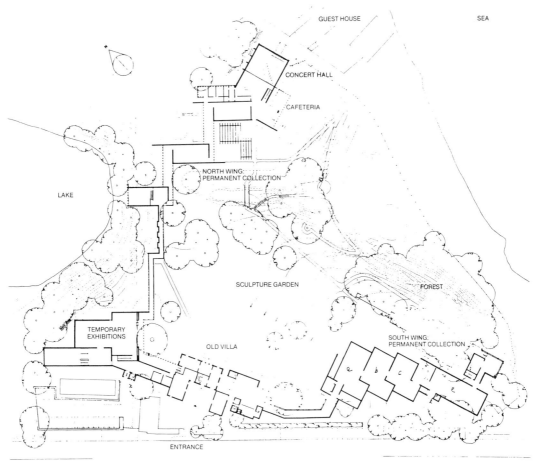

tional collection has come from the generosity of individuals and foundations. The end result seems to have been a subtle, gradual, and perhaps partly unconscious transformation. What began as a personal collection, along with certain other personal cultural enterprises that people were allowed to enjoy, has become, in the American sense of the words, a private institution dedicated to serving the public. Moreover Louisiana expects to raise private funds to carry out that purpose. For Europe, that is an extraordinary turn of events.

In 1955 Jensen purchased a small country house, built about 1850, and some twelve and a half acres of land (figs. 16, 17). The site was exceptionally beautiful, facing a small lake on one side and the coast of Sweden across the Øresund on the other. It was also well protected, by a cemetery to the northeast and a highway along the southwest border. The name Louisiana was given by the mid-nineteenth-century aristocrat who established the estate, each of whose three wives was named Louise.[21]

Upon acquisition of the house, Jensen stuffed his collections into it and selected Jørgen Bo and Vilhelm Wohlert as architects for the larger adjoining building that was to provide exhibition space. "The idea was to create an unpretentious frame around a collection of contemporary art. Louisiana's grounds with their lawns, old trees, woodland pond and view of the Sound helped to determine the architecture of the new buildings. The different aspects of the park landscape had to be retained, and in order to get a sense of it the architects . . . wandered through it for months. . . . They got to know the lie of the land through their feet, so to speak; they decided which trees were indispensable,

and they studied the path of the sun over the site."[22]

The museum was opened to the public in August 1958. The expectation was that it would attract forty thousand visitors annually; two hundred thousand came the first year and something like a quarter of a million every year since. A major temporary exhibition may draw four thousand visitors a day.[23] These figures indicate that Louisiana is the most popular museum in Scandinavia.

What one sees today are the original house built about 1850, the new museum of 1958 (now the north wing), and four more recent additions. The original architects, Bo and Wohlert, have been in charge of the design since the project began. The total area of the building is at present 94,444 square feet. At least one further addition is contemplated that will bring the whole to 116,666 square feet. It is part of the happy informality of the design that at each stage the building was coherent; no addition ever seemed an appendage.

The successive expansions reflected developing needs. Initially the museum was a small collection consisting primarily of Danish art. It emphasized temporary exhibitions and gave musical and literary performances to gain public attention. These activities had particular needs that the original galleries accommodated with difficulty. So in 1966 and again in 1971 galleries for temporary exhibitions were built north of the original house at the point where the connecting corridor breaks diagonally (fig. 17). In 1976 came a concert hall northeast of the cafeteria. These specialized quarters enabled the individual temporary performances to attain international professional standards.

Meanwhile the collections grew steadily until another wing became a necessity if the museum was to

present a representative selection of the almost five hundred works of art that, by the early eighties, constituted the permanent collections. (At that time less than half of the paintings and sculpture were Danish.) In 1982 the generosity of the Augustinus Foundation made possible the creation of a south wing for this purpose. The master plan calls for one final extension, additional rooms for temporary exhibitions, and a multipurpose room, underground, to the south of the cafeteria. These would be linked to the south wing by a subterranean corridor.

The original house is modest in scale, charming in design, and distinctively mid-nineteenth-century (fig. 16). The architects' problem was to identify functions it could perform that would make it integral to the museum. Now it serves as an entrance lobby as well as providing administrative offices, guest quarters, and a "cradle roll" where children can paint watercolors or model in clay while their parents visit the museum. Most importantly, it establishes at the start the sense of domesticity and mood of relaxation that are fundamental to the experience of visiting Louisiana.

A corridor opening from its north side proceeds in long zigs and short zags to link the house to the northern extensions (figs. 17, 18). The first extension one comes upon contains galleries for temporary exhibitions and has a film theater beneath. The second contains galleries for the permanent collections, a restaurant, and a concert hall. At a glance the plan may appear needlessly complex, but it reflects the determination both to take maximum advantage of the surroundings and in no way to injure them. Thus the opening runs of the corridor define a quasi-pentagonal court. This is in order to preserve and exploit a magnifi-

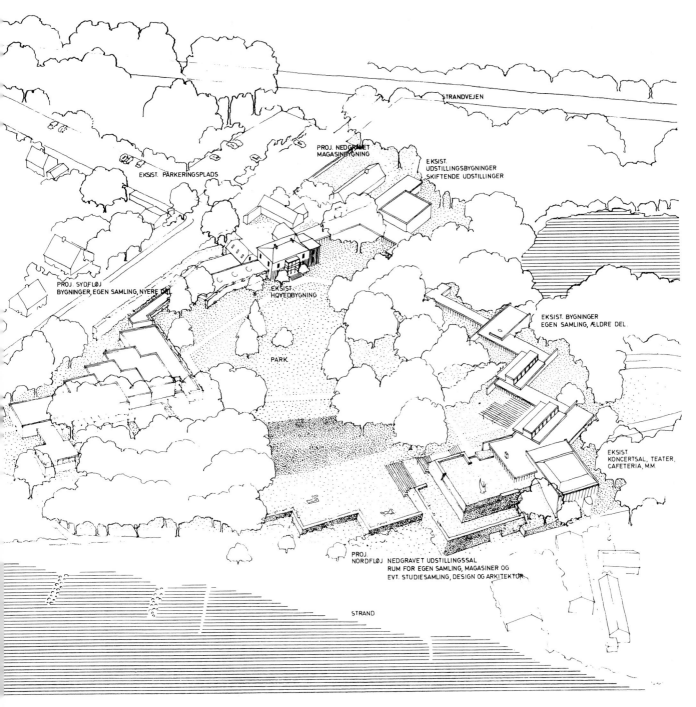

STRANDVEJEN

PROJ. NEDGRAVET
MAGASINBYGNING

EKSIST.
UDSTILLINGSBYGNINGER
SKIFTENDE UDSTILLINGER

EKSIST. PARKERINGSPLADS

PROJ. SYDFLØJ
BYGNINGER, EGEN SAMLING, NYERE DEL

EKSIST.
HOVEDBYGNING

EKSIST. BYGNINGER
EGEN SAMLING, ÆLDRE DEL

PARK

EKSIST.
KONCERTSAL, TEATER,
CAFETERIA, M.M.

PROJ.
NORDFLØJ NEDGRAVET UDSTILLINGSSAL
RUM FOR EGEN SAMLING, MAGASINER OG
EVT. STUDIESAMLING, DESIGN OG ARKITEKTUR

STRAND

18. *Louisiana. Bird's-eye view, from the east. The original villa is at top center.*

19. *Louisiana. Corridor and beech tree, northeast of the entrance. The corridor is lined with paintings on one side; the glass wall permits the visitor to admire the tree.*

20. *Louisiana. Exterior of the library-lunchroom, 1958 addition. Bo and Wohlert at their most Miesian.*

21. *Louisiana. Interior of the library-lunchroom. Designed as a library, it was the inevitable recourse of picnickers avoiding rain and gradually became a cafeteria.*

cent two-hundred-year-old beech tree with nine conjoined trunks, around which the corridor bends (figs. 17, 19). The architectural atmosphere is informal, the scale domestic, but the visitor is definitely though unobtrusively directed.

The architecture of the original galleries was inspired by Mies van der Rohe (fig. 20). They have glass walls running from their tile floors to their projecting wooden roofs. The restaurant fireplace is simply expressed (fig. 21). Throughout the handling is relaxed, though never casual. It is Mies speaking in an easy vernacular, now and then lively but inelegant, as vernacular often is.

Especially in the original construction, "the stamp of a museum—technical, dogmatic, institutional—has been deliberately avoided." This involved throughout simple materials and familiar construction: tile floors, whitewashed brick walls, ceilings carried by pine beams, and for the most part, side light. In Jensen's words: "What is more beautiful than a whitewashed wall?"[24]

But this uniformity is matched by the studied variety of the spaces.

Notable is the skillful use of diagonals in the planning. The visitor is hardly aware of a change in direction, but the shifts subtly relieve monotony and enable the architects to exploit a succession of phenomena out of doors, whether the great tree, the spread of a lawn, or the best view of the water. The original corridor, constant in its dimensions, is lit now on one side, now on both; it may be flanked by shallow niches filled with plants or sculpture, or by projecting screens carrying paintings (fig. 22). The corridor takes every possible advantage of the adjacent garden, now bordering a pool across which a trail of stones leads to a statue, now opening onto a lawn cafe with a superb panorama of the sea beyond.

Galleries are comparably diverse. The original museum seems like a bungalow. But the architects took advantage of a sharp drop in the ground level to create a startling two-story gallery with its end wall a picture window opening onto the lake (figs. 18, 23). This gallery was intended for outsize paintings. Beneath the balcony from which one enters is a gallery

without daylight intended for the display of watercolors. Two relatively large galleries in the north wing have gentle monitor lighting that concentrates illumination on the walls (fig. 24). Moreover the light is deliberately interrupted by beams that cross the space beneath the monitors. And finally comes the restaurant, a thoroughly relaxed room, formerly a library, equipped with bookshelves and an open fireplace and the finest of all the views (fig. 21).

In general, each of the original rooms was designed to accommodate with equal attractiveness a wide variety of works of art, paintings, sculptures, textiles, furniture; indeed initially the larger rooms had to be put to diverse purposes. By removing a flexible end wall, one gallery became a concert hall; when it was too cold or rainy for visitors to eat their luncheon out of doors, the original library served as a dining room.

The distribution of works of art among these somewhat dispersed galleries follows visual rather than intellectual principles. Thus sculptures by Giacometti characterize the large gallery by the lake. The original galleries to the north are now dominated by the artists associated with the Cobra group, who exerted a significant influence in Denmark. Paintings by such American artists as Andy Warhol, Roy Lichtenstein, Morris Louis, and Jim Dine are conspicuous in the new south galleries. Much of the distinguished collection of contemporary sculpture is arranged out of doors in small groups of objects by the same artist. Most "are exhibited close to the buildings so that they can be experienced from inside. The further away they are from the buildings, the weaker is their link with the architecture, and very few sculptures truly lend themselves to wholly natural landscape."[25]

Louisiana was the first significant commission of its architects. Of course their style has evolved during the past quarter century. An important change as Louisiana developed was the use of skylights in the galleries of the south wing, instead of the monitors used earlier. The new rooms have therefore unbroken warm gray floors and unbroken light walls; long strips of uniform glass constitute the almost unbroken ceilings. The exterior presents a succession of simple brick prisms, except for the terminal room, a place of relaxation, whose continuously windowed walls look out over the sea. Its exterior elevation recalls Frank Lloyd Wright rather than Mies.

Appropriately in a Danish building, one distinction of the museum buildings is the quality of the decorative arts. There has been a conspicuous attempt to assemble the finest contemporary Danish products and to arrange attractive rest areas where textiles and furniture can be enjoyed. Complementary is the attention given to essential objects in the building itself, from door handles to light shades. What is notable in the fi-

nal result is the lack of assertiveness of all these objects; they never create the impression of self-conscious display, rather they quietly enhance the total visual experience.

Louisiana is the only modern museum whose architecture I have never heard criticized by anyone who has seen it.

Of importance almost equal to the building is the treatment of the landscape. The distinctive natural features are enhanced, for example, by placing a wooden viewing stand at a suitable point overlooking the sea. Man-made alterations have been fully preserved, like the splendid lawns. Above all, the estate has been enriched with statuary. With variety and sensitivity the great pieces by Henry Moore and Alexander Calder have been placed near the shore (fig. 21), while the Arps and a Max Bill are skillfully related both to the buildings and to appropriate trees and shrubs. Louisiana has perhaps the most successful public sculpture garden yet created.[26]

Any such description as this necessarily misrepresents Louisiana precisely by stressing its excellences. Yet the purpose of the museum is not to provide a vivid, but rather an enduring experience. The very diversity of appeals implies devoting quite a little time to your visit.

The museum is a private institution controlled by a self-elective board of trustees, although appointments to the board are approved by the Ministry for Cultural Affairs. Mr. Jensen is chairman of the board. The state contributed forty percent of the costs of the original construction. "Louisiana receives state aid from the Ministry for Cultural Affairs and local subsidies from the municipality of greater Copenhagen. These grants supply (as of 1982) three million

kroner [about $430,000] towards the running costs; a further three million kroner revenue is derived from admissions and sales. Any loss is covered by the Louisiana Foundation."[27] Were additional income needed, the enthusiasm for the institution is so widespread that somehow, somewhere the funds would be found. To an outsider the museum seems well but not lavishly maintained. There are impressive economies. The beautiful gardens contain no flowers.

Most acquisitions have been purchased by the Foundation—of which likewise Mr. Jensen is chairman. Obviously there has never been the money to acquire the costly classics of twentieth-century art. There is but one painting by Picasso, none by Braque or Klee; no statues by Brancusi. But prompt recognition of quality, alertness, and ingenuity have enabled the museum to acquire an impressive collection of works by leading artists of the next generation, notably sculpture by Giacometti, Calder, Henry Moore, and Arp.

Knud Jensen does not think of Louisiana in isolation. His point of departure (like Mrs. Gardner's) was his dislike of conventional museums. "Most of them were built in one of the architectural Dark Ages—in the ambitious, bourgeois style of the last century with masses of columns and marble staircases—pompous and mindless prestige architecture." But his objections extend deeper than building style. "We are living in a period in which the task of the museum in its community is no longer the purely traditional one to conserve, to store and to display works of art in the somewhat sterile spirit inherited from the nineteenth century which created the lifeless, formal and somewhat priggish conception of what a museum should be."[28]

He therefore does not believe in

22. *Louisiana. Corridor with paintings, 1958 addition.*

23. *Louisiana. Giacometti gallery, 1958 addition. The visitor at the end of a long corridor turns left to find himself on a balcony looking down into a deep room, and beyond, still deeper, the water.*

expanding the grand old institutions. Instead a metropolis should be served by a chain of smaller museums located in the suburbs, the dormitory towns, or out in the country. Each of these new small museums could specialize in some particular period or aspect of art history. They could become local cultural centers and also objectives for that part of the population that feels it must get out of town on weekends. Operating costs could be met, as at Louisiana, from a variety of sources.[29]

This is a challenging proposal. It does raise two problems. Since the old central museums would presumably have to be maintained, if only for storage, the increase in tax and other moneys devoted to museums would be considerable. The success of Louisiana depends on Mr. Jensen's exceptional abilities. How effective would a series of small museums be if they were run by directors of average talents?

The cumulative record of the various small museums dotted about greater London has not been impressive.

24. *Louisiana. Monitor-lit gallery, 1958 addition. The deep and closely spaced wooden beams recall familiar American building practice, though their use in combination with painted brick walls and a monitor roof is surprising.*

The Yale Center for British Art

Paul Mellon epitomizes the truly great collector.[30] He began collecting casually, but came to recognize that British art was important and much neglected. In the end he determined to assemble a comprehensive visual survey of English art, life, and thought from the early seventeenth century to about 1850.

He has written: "My father was a collector of English, Dutch and Barbizon School paintings, and within the confines of a large, dark Victorian house in a very murky and gloomy city [Pittsburgh], these paintings, lighted by their gooseneck reflectors, shone out like softly lit jewels, and gave off an aura of warmth and friendliness. My mother was English, and between my birth in 1907 and the first War, I was taken to England every summer."[31]

At high school Mellon came to love English literature; at Yale he studied under an extraordinary group of scholar-teachers dedicated to English history and culture. Two years at Cambridge followed, where he cultivated other enthusiasms, especially fox hunting and horse racing. In 1931 he started purchasing color-plate books and books on racing and hunting. A few years later he bought a few paintings. After the second World War he began to collect more seriously.

In the late 1950s the Virginia Museum of Fine Arts proposed to arrange an exhibition on "Sport and the Horse," and Mellon agreed to head the selection committee. This responsibility brought him into touch with the English expert Basil Taylor. They became friends and his enthusiasm for collecting English art grew by leaps and bounds. Mellon writes: "It was he [Taylor] also who opened up my eyes to the beauty and freshness of English drawings and water-colors, their immediacy and sureness of technique, their comprehensiveness of subject matter, their vital qualities, their Englishness." Eventually the two men evolved an amateur partnership in what was to become "the most massive example of selective buying . . . in the history of collecting."[32] Today, no single institution, even in England, can match the range of the Mellon collection within the centuries of his choice.

The extent is astounding: more than 1,200 oil paintings, 10,000 drawings, 20,000 prints, 20,000 rare books, a substantial reference library, and a quarter of a million photographs.[33] Mellon's purpose in assembling so much was "to persuade scholars, critics, and the public that British art is manifold, curiously happy, and far more comprehensive than generally realized. And of a special order of excellence." His hope is "that this unique combination of materials will encourage scholars to attempt to see English civilization in its wholeness, to embark on interdisciplinary studies which will relate separate branches of learning one to another."[34]

The above suggests a very institutional assemblage. In fact, the Mellon collection has a strong personality. There are a few great English portraits by the familiar eighteenth-century masters, but conspicuous is Mellon's "passion for small paintings, representations of the English countryside in watercolors, and scenes of the world of the horse, of hunting and racing."[35] These general traits are joined to a particular enthusiasm for individual artists, notably George Stubbs and William Blake.

By the mid-1960s Mellon began to think about the ultimate disposition of his collection. Though he was associated with both our National Gallery and the Virginia Museum of Fine Arts, he concluded that "the ferment of a university would enliven and stimulate the study of and the enjoyment of these artistic relics . . . more vitally and more resourcefully than if they were passively displayed in a non-teaching institution."[36] Yale's intellectual tradition made it the obvious choice. Late in 1966 he offered Yale the collection, and funds to build a suitable building, as well as an endowment not only to run that building but also to finance fellowships, teachers, and research in British culture. Finally he asked that his name should not be attached to the Yale Center for British Art.

Mellon continued to collect British art, but with a change in emphasis. He tried, wherever possible, to add paintings, drawings, and books of recognized stature, such as Turner's *Dort Packet Boat*, Stubbs' four great shooting paintings, and a Rubens sketch for the ceiling of the Whitehall Banqueting House. Also he acquired more works by sixteenth- and seventeenth-century English artists.

But the responsibility for fulfilling his intentions passed to New Haven. A faculty committee spent 1967 considering how to make the optimum use of the Mellon collection. One refreshing innovation was the involvement of undergraduates in the planning. Jules Prown, a Yale art historian, became director in July 1968. He selected Louis Kahn of Philadelphia as architect, whose final building the Center proved to be. Another year of study was devoted to defining the program for the building. Kahn began work early in the autumn of 1969.

Important in Prown's choice of Kahn was the architect's success as a designer of art museums. His first

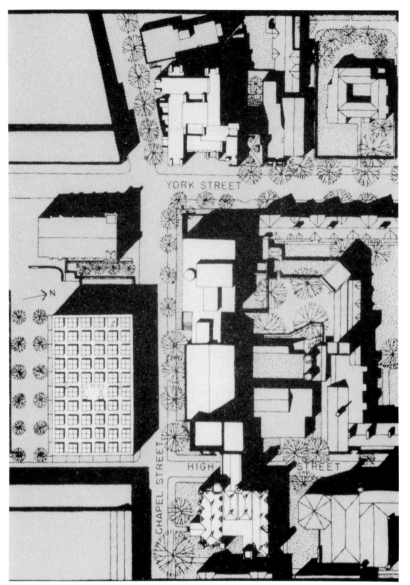

25. *Yale Center for British Art, New Haven, Connecticut, completed 1976; architect Louis Kahn. Site plan. The British Art Center is the rectangular block at left center; other Yale art buildings are highlighted in white.*

had been the extension of the Yale Art Gallery, across the street from the site of the new museum; his most recent the widely acclaimed Kimbell Art Museum in Fort Worth. That one-story building stands on a generous lot in a park-like area made up of similar public buildings each in its own ample space. Kahn's solution there was a series of uniform, parallel, barrel-vaulted corridors. Because of Kahn's mastery of proportions and the concern he devoted to controlling Texas' intense sunlight these corridors proved admirably adapted not only to the display of a variety of works of art but also to the diverse activities that take place in every lively art museum.

At the Yale Center Kahn confronted several problems he had not faced at the Kimbell. The audience was more homogeneous, basically academics ranging from school children to retired scholars, but most visitors were individually committed to one aspect or another of the Center's large collection. Finally Kahn had a restricted, midcity site. Obviously he could not repeat the Kimbell. What he achieved was a masterpiece of urban design and a building with a diversity of interiors, the best of which are unexcelled.

The site obtained for the building is a corner lot on the south side of Chapel Street, which establishes the south side of the Yale campus (fig. 25). Directly across from the Center are the two units of the Yale Art Gallery, diagonally east the History of Art Department, diagonally west the School of Art and Architecture. Immediately adjacent to the west is a former church, now the home of the Yale Repertory Theater. The British Art Center is the largest building of this disparate group, and, significantly, the simplest.

Functionally the location could not have been surpassed. Politi-

cally there was a problem. Along Chapel Street was a row of shops. To remove these would narrow the city's tax base. While the faculty were planning, the administration was negotiating. They agreed to retain a series of shops along Chapel Street and added a restaurant that is set back from the street between the Center's building and the theater. The new stores paid fifty percent more in taxes than those they replaced.

A visit to the British Art Center is a succession of disjunctive architectural experiences. One never implies another or leads into another; each is complete in itself and one moves on impelled only by curiosity. Wholly lacking is that almost imperceptible sense that one is being directed that pervades Louisiana. It is only perhaps on a

third visit that one becomes aware of deliberately contrasting experiences or of experiences repeated or more likely inverted. But these are intriguing ingenuities. As in a book of short stories, the essence is each experience in itself.

The exterior is deceptively simple (fig. 26). A concrete frame defines a four-story rectangular block. The columns are twenty feet apart. The floors linking them are expressed as concrete beams, but the pattern of rectangles varies, reflecting the arrangements of the rooms within. Along Chapel and High Streets there are shops, so every other column is omitted on the ground floor and the linking beam is deeper than usual. Because here and only here the windows are inset, one is much more aware of the beam's thickness. The heavier

26. *Yale Center. Exterior from the northeast. One enters through the open space behind the "One Way" arrow. The top-floor window right of the corner throws side light on Turner's Dort Packet Boat (fig. 37).*

ground-floor beam is repeated at the roof line, but here it is beveled inward. At a slight distance one can also see the inward slope of the concrete base that supports the skylights. In places on three sides the linking beam at third-floor level is omitted, indicating a two-story reading room within.

The infill consists of great sheets of stainless steel, the color of pewter, set flush with the skeleton. Each bends outward at floor level to provide a drip molding; many bend inward around the almost frameless windows. These come in half a dozen rectangular shapes, at the east end arranged with strict regularity, elsewhere in casual diversity. The windows vividly reflect the buildings across the street, or the sky. While it was still being designed Kahn was asked about the color of the building: "On a gray day it will look like a moth; on a sunny day like a butterfly," he replied.[37] The dominant note established by the regular skeleton and the harmonious proportions is classic calm. Solemnity, dignity, serenity, how quickly these Augustan virtues spring to mind.

The five university art buildings lining Chapel Street are similar in scale but differ remarkably in character. The Center pulls all together in an astonishing way. Very much a block, it echoes the blockiness of Addison Swartwout's Art Gallery across the street. Its affirmative horizontals recall the linear indentations in the all-but-freestanding wall of the Art Gallery extension further up the street. Kahn himself had designed this two decades earlier. The Center's planar surfaces throw into terminal relief the thrusting verticals of Paul Rudolph's Art and Architecture building. In short, Kahn's final design has created one of the most stimulating and gratifying street blocks in America. Unfortunately no photograph can do it justice.

One is overwhelmingly aware of the building as an entity, drawn in upon itself. Nothing suggests a building intended to serve the public directly. Rather it might be a factory or a laboratory devoted if not to secret work, then to some arcane endeavor. But the effect is admirably light-hearted. The building does not take itself too seriously.

From most approaches, the building does not appear to have an entrance. At first visit it does seem odd that one shop is missing, and this at the most important corner. The dark hole tempts one to investigate, and indeed near the inner corner of this large, low, dark, and almost empty space there is a modest door, discreetly titled.

That passed through, the visitor finds himself in another large square, a shaft of space, more well than courtyard, "austere" to some, "bleak" to others. The concrete skeleton is repeated, with infill panels, of steel at the ground floor, of white oak above. Occasional openings interrupt the panels but give little impression of what lies behind. Rarely a guard will spy down at you from one of these. It is all too easy to identify with the single work of art in the midst of this forty-by-forty-foot space, a slender, squirming leaden statue of William III (fig. 27).

Nothing so far experienced suggests the complexity of the program that was presented to Louis Kahn. There were three large collections: rare books; paintings; and drawings, watercolors, photographs, and prints. Part of each was to be separately exhibited and the remainder so stored as to be ideally accessible to scholars. A couple of seminar rooms were needed, and an auditorium to seat more than two hundred. The latter had to be accessible to the public at night after the museum had

closed. Since an active program of temporary exhibitions was envisaged, all of the usual museum service areas had to be provided—parking, offices, workshops, a conservation laboratory for works of art on paper, and finally as many shops as possible, partly to provide income from rents, partly to preserve an active commercial street, and, of course, to pay taxes.

Kahn's *parti* is brilliant, in essence a rectangular figure eight with galleries enclosing the eastern courtyard and three interconnecting libraries around that to the west (figs. 28, 29). Two choices governed much of the interior design, a strong preference for natural light and a desire for roomlike spaces. So keen was Kahn on effects of domesticity that it is said he even considered installing fireplaces in some of the galleries.[38]

The building does not fill the entire site, so there is space for parking at the rear (fig. 25). The basement accommodates physical plant, workshops, and washrooms, in addition to providing storage for part of the painting collection. Another portion is occupied by the stage and the steeply descending seats of the auditorium (fig. 30). Immediately to the west of the Center, a grand flight of steps leads down from the street to a sunken court onto which the restaurant faces. But the court can also provide evening access to the auditorium through a door at the side of the stage.

On the ground floor shops line the two streets, except for the corner vestibule. The eastern shaft of space rises a full four stories, while to the west the ground floor is occupied by the upper portion of the auditorium. Between these two is a low-studded shadowed space given over to the sales desk, elevators, and a circular stair. At the southwest corner of the building are twin delivery bays for trucks, one

27. *Yale Center. Entrance court. The windows to the galleries are equipped with metal fire screens that slide down grooves in the columns. The ground-floor area to the right (actually not this dark) leads to the information desk, the lecture hall stairs, and the elevators.*

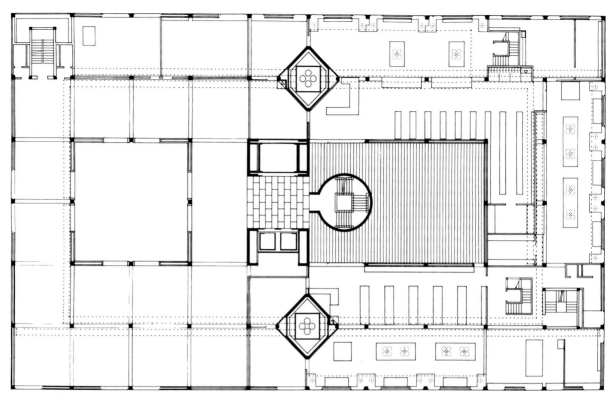

to serve the museum, the other for the shops on Chapel Street.

On the second floor the eastern court is ringed by galleries for temporary exhibitions, while to the west, over the auditorium, a second court rises three floors to the skylights (fig. 31). Paneled in white oak, hung with large paintings, carpeted, equipped with luxurious sofas, this recalls to some observers the great hall of a stately English country house. The impression is jarred by the concrete silo that houses the main stair (fig. 32). It had been Kahn's intention to enclose the stair in glass. This was not permitted under the rigorous building regulations of New Haven. But the essence of the Yale Center depends upon the contrast between the elegantly detailed concrete skeleton and the lavish materials of the simple infilling panels. The appearance in this space of a huge concrete cylinder is daunting.

This court is ringed on three

sides by low-seeming stacks, from which one passes to three two-story reading rooms along the outer walls of the building (fig. 33). These are surrounded by balconies that link together the parts of a second floor of stacks. Each reading room is an intimate space, attractive in proportions; it unites large windows, white oak furnishings of remarkable simplicity, aggressive metal chandeliers, and "enormous, silvery, cylindrical ducts, worthy of High Tech's shiniest fantasies."[39] Everybody pays a high aesthetic price for Kahn's allegiance to a straightforward treatment of all mechanical elements. The effect of these ducts is even more harmful in many of the galleries, especially those on the third floor, where they quite overwhelm the drawings and prints for the display of which that space was intended.

But the glory of the Yale Center is the galleries that surround both courts on the top floor (fig. 34).

28. *Yale Center. Second-floor plan. The entrance court is on the left, surrounded by galleries for temporary exhibitions. In the center is a passageway with a freight elevator on one side and two passenger elevators on the other. (The adjacent diamond-shaped spaces contain ducts, notably for air conditioning.) Immediately to the right of the elevators is the rectangular main stairway embedded in a concrete cylinder. Surrounding the cylinder is the library court, whose floor forms the ceiling of the lecture hall. Around this court are three separate libraries, each with reading tables near the outer wall and a double floor of stacks near the court.*

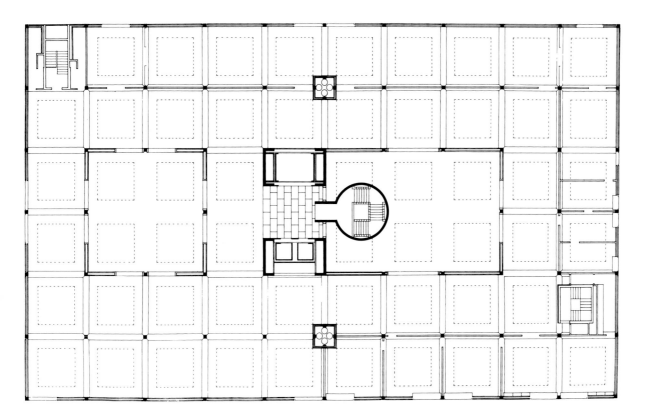

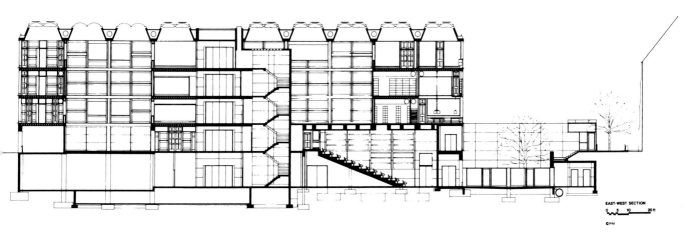

29. *Yale Center. Fourth-floor plan. Most of this floor is flexible exhibition space for paintings in the permanent collection. The reserve collection of paintings occupies seven bays at the rear, with an office at either end; other offices are along the entire west (right-hand) end of the building and the west half of the north side.*

30. *Yale Center. Longitudinal section. At the far right is the outline of the church-theater, then the sunken plaza and the restaurant building. At the right in the Art Center proper is the lecture hall with the libraries and library court above; at the left are stairs, elevators, and entrance court surrounded by bays of galleries.*

31

31. *Yale Center. Library court, looking west.*

32. *Yale Center. Library court, looking east. The beautiful proportions, the straightforward cylinder, and the regular rectangular openings suggest a study of pure geometric forms. Into this the tree, couches, and carpet make an unseemly intrusion.*

33. *Yale Center. The library: a reading room and stacks.*

34. *Yale Center. Painting galleries on the top floor. The partitions are temporary and can be moved relatively easily. The angle of the photograph unfairly suggests a boxlike character to the galleries; this can be avoided.*

35. *Yale Center. Painting reserve, at the back of the top floor.*

34

35

37

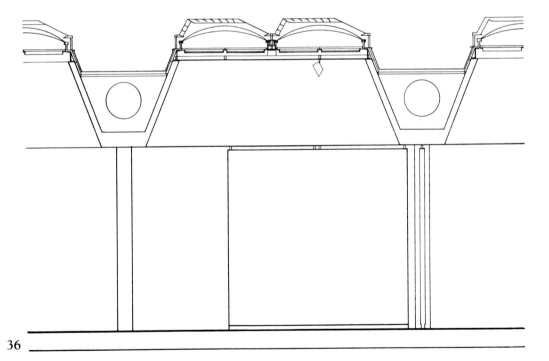

36

36. *Yale Center. Section through
fourth-floor bay and skylights.*

37. *Yale Center. Turner's* Dort
Packet Boat, *fourth floor.*

They may be the most satisfactory galleries in existence for the display of oil paintings of small to medium size. Basically the galleries consist of elegant concrete columns twenty feet apart in both directions that carry deep V-beams crowned by skylights. The square bays are separated at will by thin temporary panels that do not touch the columns. Here, even more than elsewhere, the muted richness of the materials plays an important part in the total effect. The floors are covered with a natural wool carpet, beige in color, with strips of travertine running from column to column; the walls are hung with linen; the finish is white oak. Especially remarkable is the delicacy and skill with which Kahn juxtaposes these substances. The modular exhibition spaces might seem inflexible; in actuality a considerable variety of spatial effects is possible. They make one critic "think of the lighted rooms behind rooms of seventeenth-century Dutch interiors with their pictures on the walls."[40] Considering the nature of Paul Mellon's collection of pictures, the domestic intimacy of scale here achieved is altogether admirable.

A sequence of seven bays at the rear of the building is fitted as a study gallery for the reserve collection of paintings (fig. 35). Some five hundred of them are hung frame to frame from floor to ceiling and arranged roughly by subject matter. East of this sequence is a bay containing the registrar's office. "The location of the registrar's office adjacent to the exhibition area . . . allows for ease of access by students and curatorial staff—an important feature in a study museum."[41] One bay at each end is used as an office. Publicly accessible study storage of paintings had been tried before, notably at Brooklyn and the National Gallery in London. In neither place

has the arrangement been so pleasant or so convenient for students, both visually and intellectually.

Great effort was expended on the design of the skylights (fig. 36). The final solution was only achieved after Kahn's death and reflects remarkable collaboration between the architects who succeeded him, the foreman in charge of construction, and the lighting expert. The objective was to light all walls equally at all times on any given day. The solution was tripartite: a series of vanes sloped to equalize the volume of light admitted at different seasons and times of day; a double plexiglass dome screening out ultraviolet light; and a flat ceiling of acrylic prismatic lenses directing the light toward the walls.

Overhead light is supplemented by windows looking out on the streets and by shuttered openings that provide attractive views across or down into the court. The advantage is twofold; it relates the somewhat precious experience of studying a picture to everyday reality, and it supplements the faintly clinical illumination provided by the best of skylights with the freely varying side light by which most paintings were meant to be seen. The Yale Center has been the subject of a monograph, chapters in a number of books, and something like a score of professional articles. Yet only Vincent Scully discussing these galleries has written about the most important aspect of all, what this museum does for the works of art it displays:

The climax, and I think there is one, occurs at the northeast corner, high above the entrance void [fig. 37]. There Turner's great yellow shining view of the Dort packet-boat, his homage to Cuyp, is hung. Its skylight bathes it, the slanting slabs canopy it, and one of the panes

of facade glass flanks it too, just about at its own majestic scale. . . . The light off the great Dort draws us and, reciprocally, directs our attention to the enormous window beside it. . . . It is a view of all of Kahn's predecessors in the building programs for the arts at Yale, himself in middle age among them. And sitting in front of the great Turner with its fat boat becalmed . . . one thinks once again about how Kahn chose to confront that range of buildings on the street.[42]

This painting, which Constable characterized as "the most complete work of genius I ever saw," deserves all that Kahn was able to do for it.

The Gardner, the Johnson, Louisiana, and the Yale Center are distinguished from most art museums by their clarity of purpose. They provide contrasting answers to the fundamental problem of art museums: which matters most, what a museum has or what a museum does? To phrase the problem differently: how should what a museum does relate to what it has?

It is intriguing that in their varying analyses of the art museum "situation" each of the central policy makers vividly and derogatively (though unwittingly) expresses an opinion of the others. Fenway Court is dedicated to what it has. Mrs. Gardner's will very seriously limits what it can do. So it epitomizes to perfection "the formal and somewhat priggish concept of what a museum should be" that Mr. Jensen abhors.

For him, all-important is what a museum does, and you do what seems most necessary, without much relation to what you have. The one basic museum activity he mentions rarely, and then vaguely, is acquisition. "To build up a collection of work created after 1950." Why 1950? Because starting when Jensen did with the funds then available to him he could only afford strictly contemporary objects? Or does he believe that 1950 signals the start of a new artistic epoch? "More than one piece by each" of a few favored art-

ists results notably in several impressive Henry Moores, a number of large Alexander Calders, and no less than fourteen Giacomettis. Splendid! But what are the limits of "work?" Does it include decorative art, especially non-Danish decorative art, an Eames chair, for example? In this area, has the distinction between the normal limits of a privately chosen collection and an institution's more widely representational goals been thought through? One wonders if Louisiana would accept in its entirety a distinguished collection formed by a foreigner.

It is acquisition, perhaps, that most profoundly distinguishes the Gardner from the Yale Center. Both reflect the taste of their respective founders, "but whereas Fenway Court is a monument to that taste, the Center's founder was, from the outset, anxious to suppress his own identity in favor of the works of art he collected. Individually, many of his paintings command respect, as do isolated masterpieces anywhere, but collectively they provide . . . a unique body of evidence for the study of a single culture. Just as this consideration weighed with Paul Mellon and helped him identify Yale as a suitable home for his collections, so it was reflected by Kahn in his design of a building which is both public and private, which accommodates large numbers of

general visitors and caters to the individual needs of specialists in the field."[43]

That the Yale Center "should enhance the life of the University" may be the official definition of its aims; it is not an adequate description of its accomplishments. One of the best things it has done, and consistently, is to advance knowledge by sponsoring scholarly exhibitions and publications and by subsidizing research. Yet, ultimately, the Yale Center can only strike a successful balance between having, getting, and doing if it can live happily with the fact that it is concerned with a narrower range of subject matter than the other museums discussed.

·II·
When the Architect Has His Way

The need for art museums in this country was intensified in the twentieth century by the combination of enthusiastic private purchasing of works of art and tax laws that favored the gift of this art to the public. It was therefore appropriate to begin this book with a consideration of what a few collectors have sought for the museums they created. But most private collections are given to existing public museums, and public museums have commissioned much the largest amount of art museum architecture.

The appeal of museum commissions to the greatest architects of our times is threefold. Music and the visual arts need not be political and can be the great secular spiritual values of our times. They are also popular. Compared to music, with the attendant mysteries of acoustics, works of art make few technical demands of their architects. So the idea of designing an art museum is appealing because it presents the opportunity to create an almost pure form that will serve a purpose both spiritual and democratic. What a contrast to, what a relief from the kinds of problems involved in the design of hospitals or low-cost housing!

It is logical then to devote a chapter to the art museums created by the four most influential architects of the mid-twentieth century: Wright, Le Corbusier, Gropius, and Mies van der Rohe.

Museums designed by great architects are likely to have certain features in common. The process of persuading the great and busy man to accept the commission may be difficult and involve several people. Persuading various city commissions to accept his radical proposals is almost invariably complex and likely to involve another group of people, those with political influence. Little is written down, and it usually becomes im-

possible for the historian to determine, among various claimants, who first had the happy idea, who determined the program, and who made the success of the project possible.

Because the architect is likely to have been chosen for his demonstrated interest in works of art, and because he was invited, he is more than usually sure of the rightness of his own ideas. These generally involve convictions about display and concern for the vast numbers of an unanalyzed public who he imagines will come to admire his building and glance at its contents. Brushed aside frequently are the practical considerations proposed by the professional staff. Revealing is a letter of October 13, 1950, from Frank Lloyd Wright to the director of the Guggenheim Museum: "S.O.S. It is now apparent that we cannot build Solomon R. Guggenheim's Memorial and at the same time build whole big buildings for carpentry, photography, storage, conservation, etc. etc."[1] James Johnson Sweeney got so little of these spaces that the top galleries, which Wright considered "the great features of the building," had to be closed to the public and used for the storage of those paintings there were not galleries enough to exhibit.

The Guggenheim likewise illustrates the previous point. We know neither how Wright came to be chosen as architect, who gave him what instructions, nor how closely he adhered to them. It seems appropriate, therefore, to begin with the patron in whose honor the building is named.

Frank Lloyd Wright and the Guggenheim

Of the Guggenheim it must be said that no other museum in modern times houses a private collection of such distinction in a building of such distinction.[2] Because the founder's personality now seems pale, it may have been too easy to deny him a significant contribution. Reconsidered, the direction of his artistic interest, his dedication to it, his choice of artistic collaborators, and the unwavering support he seems to have given them, all are extraordinary. Extraordinary, too, is his followers' determination and success in maintaining the standards he established.

Solomon R. Guggenheim was the fourth of eight brothers, and the youngest of the quartet who actually managed the family partnership. He was elegant, outgoing, and, at least day to day, the spokesman for the partnership. Perhaps it was in 1930 that he and his wife called on Walter Gropius at his home in Berlin. In the course of conversation about modern art and architecture Gropius asked Guggenheim why he was

38. *Solomon R. Guggenheim Museum, New York, completed 1960; architect Frank Lloyd Wright. Plan at first level, from a drawing by Wright. At the upper right the space designated "Visitor's Lounge" is now a small restaurant. The pointed oval opposite the entrance to the Grand Gallery was a sales desk (since removed); the oval in the center is a fountain at the beginning of the ramp of galleries.*

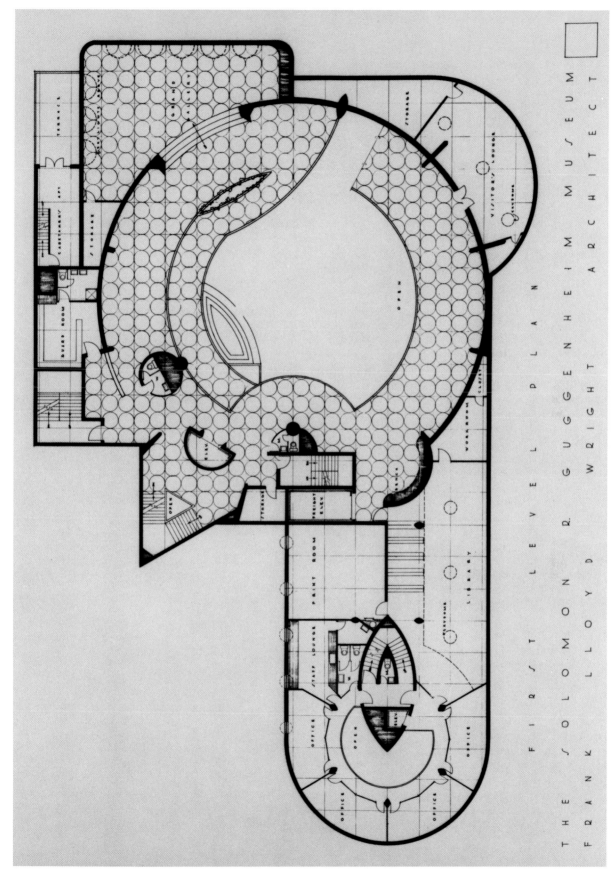

THE SOLOMON R. GUGGENHEIM MUSEUM

FRANK LLOYD WRIGHT ARCHITECT

FIRST LEVEL PLAN

39. *Guggenheim Museum. Exterior from the northwest. The extension containing offices and more exhibition space is to be built at the far left.*

collecting abstract art. As the architect reported many years later: "Apparently in early youth Guggenheim learned how serious are the obstacles a young man has to face to make his contemporaries understand new ideas. His own revolutionary ideas about the reduction and working up of copper . . . were carried through with great difficulty. So he resolved, in principle, to do everything he could to support the gifted young who sought to contribute something new, and to help them to a breakthrough."[3]

He and his wife rather modestly collected Barbizon and old master paintings for many years. In 1926, when he was sixty-five, he met Baroness Hilla Rebay von Ehrenwiesen. She had come to New York bearing a letter of introduction from his wife's sister in Paris. She was a painter, and Guggenheim insisted that she paint his portrait. With greatest reluctance she did so, for she had abandoned realism and become a passionate enthusiast for "non-objective art." She had a particular admiration for Kandinsky, and for Rudolf Bauer with whom she was deeply in love. She persuaded Guggenheim to abandon the acquisition of conventional paintings and to collect abstract art. This he proceeded to do with enthusiasm, in effect pensioning Bauer, and it is generally supposed buying everything the baroness recommended. By 1939 he had acquired some seven hundred paintings, two hundred by Bauer, one hundred by Kandinsky, others by Leger, Gleizes, Klee.

Initially the collection was hung in Guggenheim's apartment in the Plaza Hotel. In 1937 he established a foundation to which the collection was transferred, and in 1939 the foundation rented the first of a succession of quarters for a "Museum of Non-Objective Art" with the baroness as director. Dur-

ing the early forties the decision was made to build and by August 1943 the baroness had met Frank Lloyd Wright. She claimed that she had selected him for "the construction of the most important museum in the world."[4]

He submitted preliminary sketches to her and Guggenheim on July 27, 1944, and a first scheme was approved later that year. An abundance of problems ensued. Obtaining a suitable site took four years; construction during the war was impossible. Guggenheim had planned to spend $250,000 for the land and $750,000 for the building. The early designs would have cost far more than this and repeatedly had to be reduced. The eventual expenditure came to $4,212,267, and even so, "damn it, the building looked cheap," as a prominent practitioner wrote in the journal of the American Institute of Architects.[5] To satisfy the New York City building department required three years of negotiation. In all, Wright claimed to have made seven complete sets of plans. The cornerstone was laid in 1956 and the museum was open to the public on October 27, 1959—more than fifteen years after Wright began work on it.

Meanwhile, in 1949 Solomon Guggenheim had died; thereafter, under the leadership of his nephew Harry, the foundation's board of trustees played an active role in everything to do with the museum. The name of the institution was changed to the Solomon R. Guggenheim Museum. The baroness was forced to retire in 1952 and was replaced as director by James Johnson Sweeney, who differed strongly with Wright. On April 9, 1959, Wright himself died, and Sweeney completely changed the manner of hanging and lighting the paintings, as well as the color of the interior walls.

The building extends from 88th

to 89th Street along Fifth Avenue, occupying a lot 202 by 128 feet (fig. 38). It consists of two freestanding circular towers, the larger for galleries, the smaller for offices. Both have glazed courts, the larger being ringed by a helical ramp, the smaller by circular corridors giving access to rooms along the building's perimeter (figs. 38, 40, 41). Attached to each major block is a turret, triangular in plan, containing stairs and an elevator. Cantilevered out at the second-floor level is a one-story band that unites the two towers and projects beyond the larger one to the edges of the lot along 88th Street (figs. 39, 40). In this space are a variety of rooms, notably a gallery in the area linking the towers for a special collection of paintings donated by Justin Thannhauser and a high gallery for large paintings at the southeastern corner of the lot.

The dominant, the unforgettable feature is the circular central court of the larger tower surrounded by its six stories of spiraling ramps (figs. 42, 43): "a lightflooded cathedral with a roadway to heaven winding round its walls."[6] The diameter of the inner spiral, defined by the parapet of the ramps, decreases slightly towards the top, but the diameter of the outer spiral, that is the outside wall of the building, increases markedly as it rises, so the width of the ramp is much greater at the top (fig. 40). But projecting inward at right angles to the outer surface are web walls that divide each circuit of the ramp into a series of three-sided rooms (fig. 43). It is here that the paintings are displayed, projected outward from the encircling wall or hung against the webs that extend from the outside walls toward the ramp. They are lit by the skylight covering the court and by artificial light projected down from the ceiling. Basic to Wright's thinking was that the

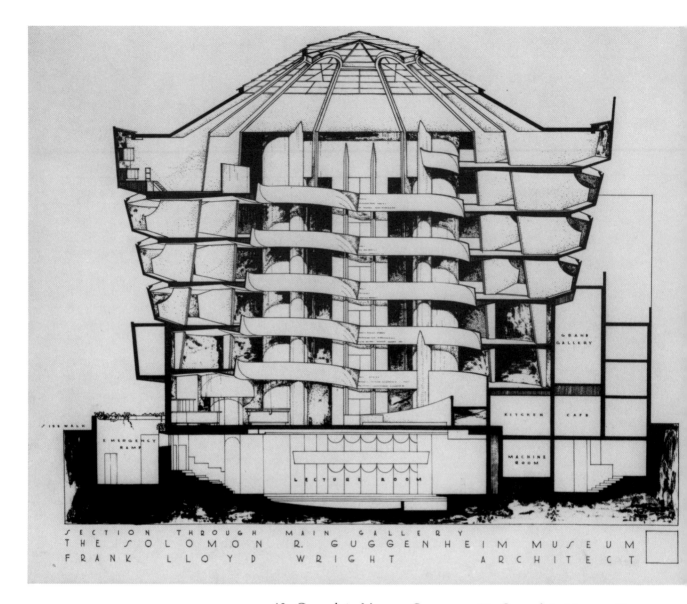

SECTION THROUGH MAIN GALLERY
THE SOLOMON R. GUGGENHEIM MUSEUM
FRANK LLOYD WRIGHT ARCHITECT

40. *Guggenheim Museum. Cross section of the main building, from a drawing by Wright. The drawing makes vivid how the total building expands as it rises, though the court diminishes so that the gallery areas grow progressively larger. The vanes breaking the gallery into niches also grow wider as they rise, so that the niche-like character of the galleries increases markedly toward the top. The drawing illustrates the overhead lighting of the paintings that Wright projected but Sweeney changed.*

41. *Guggenheim Museum. Cross section of the administrative wing, from a drawing by Wright. Although the external walls of every floor are semicircular, as built the parapet of the upper deck is rectangular.*

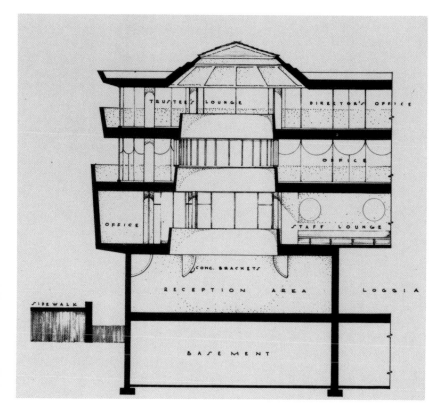

paintings must have, at most, the narrowest frames. These would not support glass, so visitors must not be allowed to approach the art too closely. To accomplish this, the sloping outer wall does not meet the ramp at the expected angle. Instead it breaks sharply inward a couple of feet above the floor. This steep slope forces the viewer to keep a respectful distance from the paintings.

Wright was nothing if not communicative and wrote so much about this museum that a double problem arises: how to sort out his ideas, and how to differentiate between an accurate description of his vision and the self-delusion of a super-salesman.

For Wright the purpose was well-defined: to create a "new unity between the beholder, painting and architecture." In a letter to Guggenheim in 1946 he referred

to the museum as "your memorial-building." These concepts established an image and a desired mood. This was to be an edifice of "great harmonious simplicity wherein human proportions are maintained . . . a reposeful place in which paintings could be seen to better advantage than they have ever been seen. . . . The nature of the building is such as to seem more like a temple in a park on the Avenue, a temple for adult education."[7]

One of the major concerns was the proper way to display paintings. In this regard the principal consideration was not the relation of the paintings to the viewers, but of the paintings to the architecture. It was assumed that "the charm of any work of art . . . is to be seen in normal, naturally-changing light." At the Guggenheim this was always to be

provided from above, whether through the central dome or the continuous bands of wall lighting at ceiling height under the outer edge of the ramps. Another principle was that the paintings should be emphasized as features in themselves. "In any right-angled room the oblong or square flat plane of a picture automatically becomes subservient to the square of the architecture. In the plastic third-dimensional sweep of the main spiral of the Guggenheim Museum any particular picture will become free to be itself; to be master of its own allotted space." "The flat plane of the picture thus detached by the curve of the wall is presented to view much as a jewel set as a signet in a ring."[8]

Wright wrote much about both the visitors and the staff. "There are many innovations in the building all on the side of convenient exposition and enjoyable social experience." He proposed motorized wheel chairs, vacuum cleaners set in the floor at every entrance to remove dirt from the visitors, and an auditorium where lantern slides could be projected onto the ceiling as well as against the walls. He expressed concern for "the people who man the museum day by day and operate it, as well as for the trustees of the museum and their friends." He thought the building would be not only convenient but flexible. "I assure you that anything you desired to happen could happen. . . . Unity of design with purpose is everywhere present."[9]

It is needless to discuss this aspect of his writing. Much of what he proposed was considered impractical or extravagant and abandoned without trial. As a museum the Guggenheim has proved difficult to operate. The paucity of space for storage has already been mentioned; Wright provided none for conservation.

Here is how Wright summarized what the individual would experience: "The gentle upward, or downward, sweep of the main spiral-ramp itself serves to make the visitors more comfortable by their very descent along the spiral, viewing the various exhibits: The elevator is doing the lifting, the visitor the drifting from alcove to alcove." A one-way transit this, past seventy-four small rooms, uniform in height and width, in effect a sequence of almost identical niches. This even sounds monotonous, but that is not the most serious shortcoming. Rather it ignores the fact that many visitors want to do something other than drift. They may wish to examine quite a number of pictures almost simultaneously, to establish how an artist evolved, for instance. Or, inspired by something seen later, they may wish to return to something seen earlier. The Guggenheim's scheme discourages these kinds of looking. But if it inhibits the visitor, it demands too much of the curator. Director James Johnson Sweeney wrote: "To enjoy to full advantage the opportunities the building offers, each level, each bay, must therefore be related to one another up and down, from level to level and across the empty center, as well as backwards and forwards along the ramp"—no light task (fig. 43).[10]

Another recurring concern is with the general nature of the building as form. Much of Wright's writing on this matter is opaque. What is one to make of this: "The basis for all picture-presentation in your memorial-building is to provide perfect plasticity of presentation?" "Plasticity" and "organic architecture" are terms whose meaning remained private to him. "This type of structure has no inside independent of the outside, as one flows with, and is of, the other. . . . This integration yields a nobility of quality and the strength of simplicity . . . a truth of which

our culture has yet seen little."[11]

The architect's writing is more satisfactory when he discusses the building more specifically. Basic to him is the contrast between "the old static architecture" and "the harmonious fluid quiet" achieved here. The Guggenheim's is an architecture of "clean, beautiful surfaces."

> The whole building, cast in concrete, is more like an egg shell—in form a great simplicity—rather than like a criss-cross structure. The light concrete flesh is rendered strong enough everywhere to do its work by embedded filaments of steel either separate or in mesh. The structural calculations are thus those of the cantilever and continuity rather than the post and beam. The net result of such construction is a greater repose, the atmosphere of the quiet unbroken wave: no meeting of the eye with abrupt changes of form. . . .
>
> Typical of the details of this edifice, symbolic figure is the oval seed-pod containing globular units. This simple figure decides the shapes of all furniture; the pedestals for sculpture, tables, flower-boxes, jardinieres, etc., etc. Features of exterior and interior, these all agree.[12]

The largest of the seed pods is the plan of the stair tower of the administration building.

The great court of the Guggenheim is an unforgettable space, at once exhilarating and pleasant. The power of the principal forms is balanced by the delightfulness of lesser elements, the seed-pod fountain, the glass wall onto the corner garden and Fifth Avenue, the friendliness of the modest and uncommercial sales desk (now gone). The space provides, moreover, an admirable background for the remarkable group of statues by Bran-

cusi that Sweeney acquired for the museum.

Visiting the Guggenheim is rewarding in human terms. Looking down and across, as one does recurrently (fig. 43), one surveys more visitors than in any other museum, sees them in motion and almost invariably looking interested and happy. Yet few consider the corridor-galleries satisfactory places to view works of art, although the intensity of criticism varies. For this viewer standing with one foot higher than another—as looking at art here requires—mildly upsets his stomach. He has to pause to recover on the patch of flat floor in front of the elevator each time around. The diminishing depth of the galleries as one descends is anticlimactic and the uniform width of the alcoves has a numbing effect. One looks forward to the variety provided by the high gallery with its irregular plan, and even anticipates the confusion of dark spaces where the Thannhauser collection hangs. In short, both positively and negatively the building obtrudes upon the experience of looking at art. And yet one constantly returns. However vividly remembered, the impact of the great space is always grander and more moving than one expected. One always discovers the excellence of hitherto unnoticed details, and even though a given exhibition may not be espe-

42. *Guggenheim Museum. Court of the main building. The interior generally presents two harmoniously contrasting images: this exceptional photograph shows only the superb and unique space, exhilarating and overpowering. Normally, as in the next illustration, there are also swarms of happy people enjoying the space from below as they circle downwards.*

cially sympathetic, one recalls each overall experience with gratification.

Frank Lloyd Wright's design for the Guggenheim had one fundamental weakness: there was no way to increase the basic exhibition space. In 1965 Justin Thannhauser loaned and in 1976 bequeathed to the museum a superlative group of French impressionist and related paintings. To accommodate them, the library, which Wright had planned as a link between the two towers, had to be turned into exhibition space, and very unsatisfactory it was.[13] In 1985 the museum announced plans for a major addi-

tion, an eleven-story rectilinear tower behind and cantilevered over the smaller of Wright's two circular towers, designed by Gwathmey Siegel & Associates. The proposal was fiercely attacked by many who saw it destroying the sculptural integrity of Wright's exterior; ultimately the proposal was reduced to a simple ten-story slab. The revised addition will still double the amount of exhibition space and provide new offices; but it will leave the museum's library, storage, and conservation space accommodated in rented quarters off the site.[14]

43. *Guggenheim Museum. View across the main court. In the galleries one can either concentrate on the works of art or move on. There need be few seats, for the Guggenheim arouses little desire to linger idly or to chat. In few public spaces are so many people so purposefully concentrated so much of the time.*

Le Corbusier in Tokyo

The lack of provision for possible expansion is a curious failure in the Guggenheim, for the idea of a museum as a contiguous spiral of corridors originated with Le Corbusier, who advocated this device precisely because it made expansion easy. In 1927 the architect had competed unsuccessfully for a building to house the League of Nations, but this had turned his thoughts to the design of vast public buildings, and to problems of world organization. In 1929 he proposed a Mundaneum, a great cultural center in Geneva. This would contain a library, a university, a sports center, but most conspicuously a World Museum.[15] This was intended to demonstrate how mankind, starting from the humblest origins, had achieved the heights of civilization.

The museum was to be a square spiral in plan, a stepped pyramid in section. The center was to be an enclosed court (fig. 44). The visitor would take a sloping elevator from the entrance to the top and then wind down the continuous corridors that spread outwards as they descended. Le Corbusier conceived the spiral as endless. If more gallery space is needed you simply advance the entrance, burrowing into the ground or wrapping the later extensions around the base of the earlier building.

In this plan each corridor consisted of three parallel paths only slightly separated. The outermost would present objects—for example Greek terra cottas, Greek busts, Greek reliefs. The central corridor would present places—the building for which those objects were created, that building's siting within its city, the city within its continent. The innermost path would present periods, that is comprehensive reconstructed images—verbal as well as visual—of the civilization of that place at that time. Thus if one followed the outermost corridor rigorously one would experience the history of art. Alternatively, if one moved horizontally across the three paths, one would experience a culture in its entirety, the object in its surroundings and both in their particular intellectual milieu.

But Le Corbusier was not simply concerned with the display of intellectual unity. He believed that by understanding various human cultures in their completeness, men would understand one another. This museum was to be a practical approach to the achievement of world peace. It was a cultural counterpart to the League of Nations as that institution was envisioned in the age of Aristide Briand.

The World Museum remained a dream. Le Corbusier repeated the spiral form to house various later dreams, for example an aesthetic center or a museum of twentieth-century art.[16] Meanwhile, beginning in 1925, he had designed a succession of small exhibition pavilions for national or international fairs. Some of these were built. In this series of designs he had experimented radically with both form and structure in buildings having about the volume of an average suburban house.

After World War II Le Corbusier was asked to design two small cultural centers in India and one in Japan. He proposed in every case a substantial art museum devoted to the permanent display of a collection. Around it he grouped three or four lesser buildings, for temporary exhibitions, for a library, for a lecture hall, for a theater, for spectacles; the precise arrangements varied. All three art museums were severe square structures with open central halls and ramps to reach the second-floor galleries. The smaller buildings by contrast were complex in form and could be unusual in structure. Invariably the governments that commissioned these complexes found Le Corbusier's proposals too expensive, and most if not all the smaller buildings were discarded. However, one small exhibition building was executed, the Centre Le Corbusier in Zurich. It vividly presents an image of what the architect had in mind as foils to the austere museums in his cultural centers.

In all three cases Le Corbusier's designs were executed locally, doubtless with varying faithfulness. He saw none of the finished buildings. Of the three, the Japanese museum was completed first, and since it houses a significant collection it best exemplifies Le Corbusier's intentions.[17]

An extraordinary story lies behind this building. The late Kojiro Matsukata was president of the Kawasaki Dockyards. Principally between 1916 and 1923 he made a collection of several thousand European paintings and sculptures.[18] Matsukata's intention was to exhibit his collection in a special museum in Japan. Prohibitive import duties delayed the carrying out of this dream. Then, unfortunately, because of the depression of 1929 most of this collection was dispersed.[19]

However, more than four hundred works were left behind in the owner's French apartment. During World War II the French government took possession of these, considering them the property of a hostile country. Under the terms of the San Francisco Peace Treaty (1951) they were declared French national property. After several years of negotiation, 308 paintings, drawings, and prints, as well as sixty-three pieces of sculpture, were given in 1959 to the government

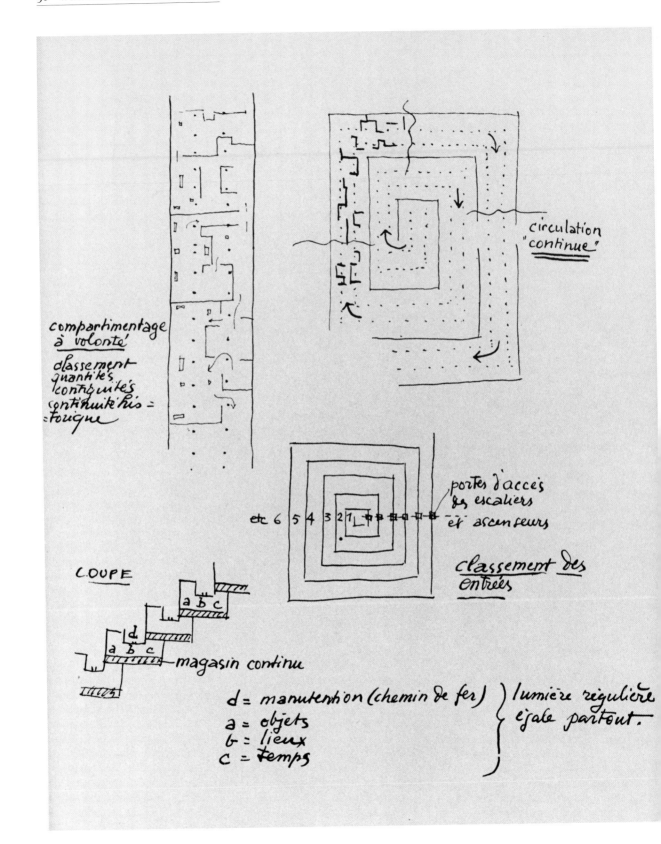

compartimentage
à volonté

classement
quantités
contiguités
continuité his=
torique

circulation
"continue"

etc 6 5 4 3 2 1   portes d'accès
des escaliers
et ascenseurs

classement des
entrées

COUPE

magasin continu

d = manutention (chemin de fer) } lumière régulière
a = objets   égale partout.
b = lieux
c = temps

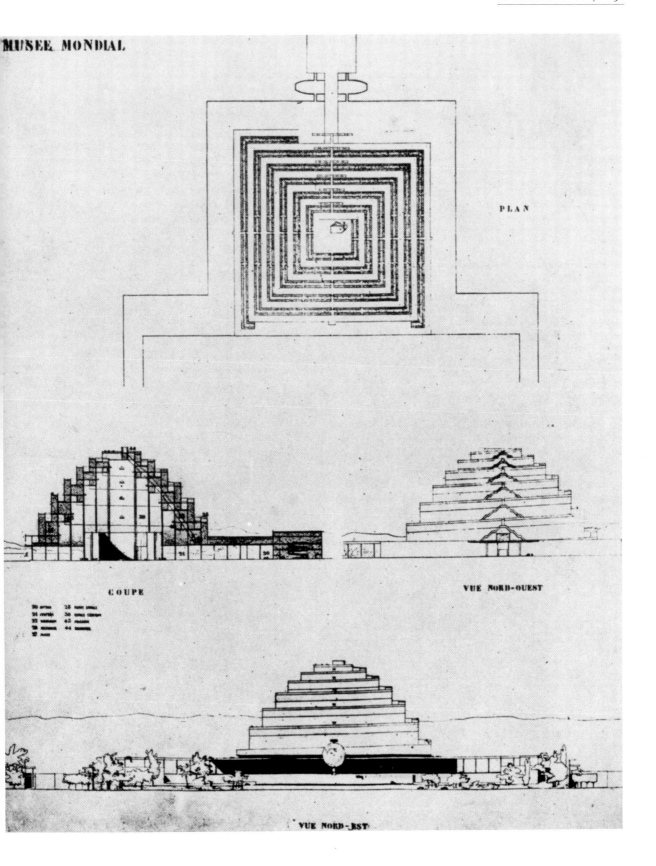

MUSÉE MONDIAL

PLAN

COUPE

VUE NORD-OUEST

VUE NORD-EST

of Japan as a token of good will. There was at least the implied condition that a special national museum would be built to house them.

The original gift included fifty-three statues by Rodin, seven paintings by Courbet, and eleven Monets, as well as works by Millet, Pissarro, Renoir, Van Gogh, Gauguin, and other French artists of the late nineteenth and early twentieth century. Since then the National Museum of Western Art has received other gifts and has purchased works of art so that the collection now comprises 931 pieces. The range is now considerably wider, including Cycladic figures and works by such artists as Rogier van der Weyden, Tintoretto, El Greco, Rubens, Goya, Picasso, and Jackson Pollock.

In the mid-1950s, thanks to the influence of "true Japanese intellectuals," Le Corbusier had been asked to design this museum. He agreed, but specified that three long-time associates, Kunio Mayekawa, Junzo Sakakura, and Takamasa Yoshizaka, should carry out the design. After more than two years of construction the building was opened in 1959. It is centrally located as one of a considerable number of important cultural buildings grouped together in Ueno Park.

(Preceding pages)

44. *Le Corbusier, proposal for a World Museum, 1929. The building is on pilotis. One proceeds from the entrance through a second-floor vestibular tube to a steeply sloping elevator. The displays begin at the top and are in a sloping corridor around an open central courtyard filled with columns. The exhibits are on rectangular screens. The corridor is divided into three lanes dealing respectively with histories of art, geography, and ideas.*

"Le Corbusier's integrated plan which covered the area surrounding the museum was beyond the scope that the Japanese government had in mind,"[20] but it is worth describing in some detail because it represents so completely what his ideal of a museum was toward the end of his life (fig. 45). There were to be four buildings within a square area defined on one side by a street. Approximately the middle third of this area, running back from the street, was to be a paved esplanade.[21] At the rear of this esplanade was a large complex consisting of an unroofed crescent of seats facing "a Box of Miracles," apparently a great stage house. Between these two units was a rectangular pool enclosing a peninsula, the stage proper.

To the right of the esplanade was a complex pavilion whose most striking feature was a pair of huge, rectangular metal "umbrellas," on contrasting axes. Doubtless the pair would have sheltered some arrangement of pavilions in which temporary exhibitions would have been installed, as is the case at the very similar Centre Le Corbusier in Zurich. Immediately adjoining were large screens for murals or posters as well as space for independent sculptural forms. Even from the dead white model it is evident that this group would have been as startling, as informal, as compelling as a county fair.

To the left, directly across the esplanade, was the box on stilts of the museum, an almost windowless masonry prism from whose second-floor doorway a massive balcony projected, with a narrow stair going down to the plaza. Adjoining, with its back to the street, there was another prismatic building, this one firm to the ground. Strikingly if drunkenly strip-windowed, it was to house a library below and a lecture hall above.

The subsidiary buildings do not seem to have been studied in great detail, but the ground plan of the museum was elaborated (fig. 46). It is as if Le Corbusier not only took pride in providing all those practical facilities that Sweeney sought in vain from Wright, but also delighted in demonstrating just how he had done so. A special stair leads down to toilets in the basement. The vestibule contains an appropriately isolated cashier's desk, a bookstore, a coatroom, and the receptionist. At the opposite end of the facade there is a lounge for visitors. In addition there is a locker room, toilets, kitchen, and lounge for the guards, not to mention a service entrance, workshops, storerooms for supplies and another for works of art. On and on, more than two dozen separate items are numbered on the ground-floor plan with a corresponding list of explicit titles beside it.

Mayekawa, Sakakura, and Yoshizaka must have been masters of diplomacy. "With Le Corbusier's permission, the museum was reduced to the smallest possible scale," some 46,000 square feet; they built it at a cost of $611,000.[22] Only the museum proper was executed, though by sacrificing some storage a library was fitted into its ground floor.[23]

It is a strictly square building, 137 feet by 137 feet, supported on concrete columns some twenty-three feet apart (fig. 47). Throughout, every dimension is determined by Le Corbusier's personal system of proportions, the *modulor*.[24] The entire front third of the ground floor is an open colonnade, admirable as a place where groups of visitors can assemble, admirable also for the display of a few of Matsukata's large collection of Rodin bronzes. The remainder of the ground floor is devoted to those practical necessities already mentioned.

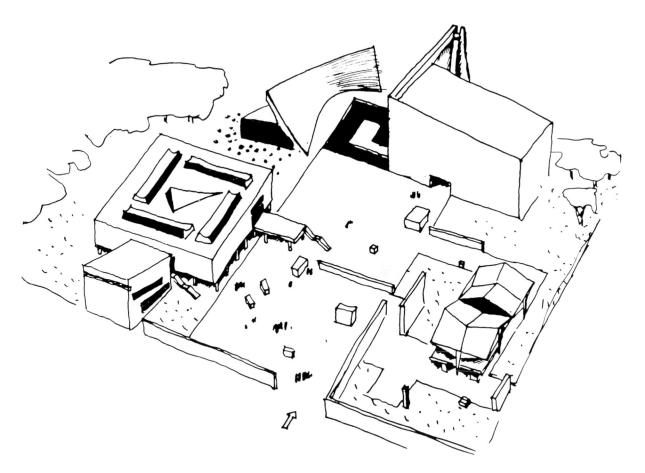

The most striking feature of the interior is a central court rising the whole height of the building (fig. 48). One third of this space is given over to a zigzag of ramps leading to the galleries. Conspicuous are two slender columns that carry a cross of delicate beams; above this an extraordinary pyramid, triangular in plan and steep in elevation, provides illumination. Presumably for aesthetic reasons, light comes into the court only from the north side of the pyramid. But the building's orientation is determined by the street outside, and its corners face the points of the compass. So, looking upwards, each side of the pyramid runs in a direction diagonal to the sides of the court. Skylight aside, all planes are untreated concrete, though Japanese craftsmen gave

this material exceptional smoothness of surface.[25] But the result differs sharply from what Le Corbusier had in mind. He proposed to cover the walls with five hundred square meters of photomurals of his own design (fig. 49).

The dominant space in most twentieth-century art museums is the multistory central court. When one enters this at the National Museum of Western Art, one's first impression is of its rightness. Harmonious in proportions, sympathetic in size, capable of accommodating a crowd, it is not an overwhelming vacuum when empty, for the scale is adjusted to the individual; it suggests that the museum will be perfectly appropriate to the easel paintings and moderate-sized sculpture that characterized the bourgeois art of the impressionist

45. *National Museum of Western Art, Tokyo, completed 1959. Le Corbusier's bird's-eye sketch of his proposal. The street at the bottom defines the edge of Ueno Park. At the top is the "Box of Miracles," at lower right a pavilion for temporary exhibitions; neither of these was built. The museum proper, as Le Corbusier envisioned it, is at the left in the drawing.*

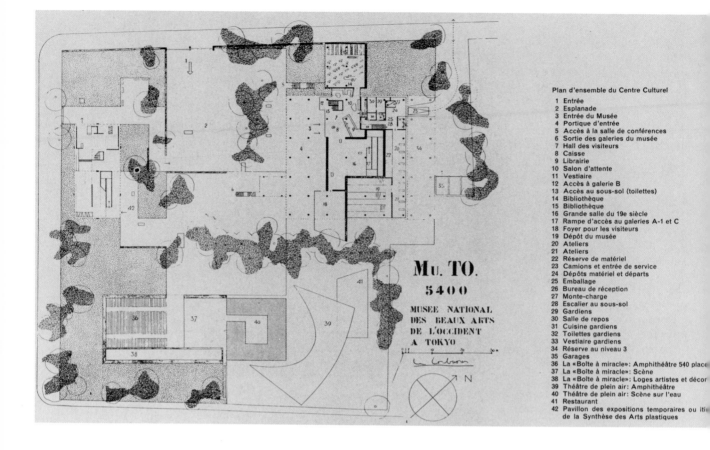

Plan d'ensemble du Centre Culturel

1 Entrée
2 Esplanade
3 Entrée du Musée
4 Portique d'entrée
5 Accès à la salle de conférences
6 Sortie des galeries du musée
7 Hall des visiteurs
8 Caisse
9 Librairie
10 Salon d'attente
11 Vestiaire
12 Accès à galerie B
13 Accès au sous-sol (toilettes)
14 Bibliothèque
15 Bibliothèque
16 Grande salle du 19e siècle
17 Rampe d'accès au galeries A-1 et C
18 Foyer pour les visiteurs
19 Dépôt du musée
20 Ateliers
21 Ateliers
22 Réserve de matériel
23 Camions et entrée de service
24 Dépôts matériel et départs
25 Emballage
26 Bureau de réception
27 Monte-charge
28 Escalier au sous-sol
29 Gardiens
30 Salle de repos
31 Cuisine gardiens
32 Toilettes gardiens
33 Vestiaire gardiens
34 Réserve au niveau 3
35 Garages
36 La «Boîte à miracle»: Amphithéâtre 540 place
37 La «Boîte à miracle»: Scène
38 La «Boîte à miracle»: Loges artistes et décor
39 Théâtre de plein air: Amphithéâtre
40 Théâtre de plein air: Scène sur l'eau
41 Restaurant
42 Pavillon des expositions temporaires ou iti
de la Synthèse des Arts plastiques

46. *National Museum of Western Art. Plan of the projected ensemble; the museum is at upper right, an approximate square defined by dots. In all essentials the latter was built as here shown. The proposed wing at top was added later to a modified design. The left third of the ground floor is open, performing the same diversity of functions as the introductory hall of major American museums; below the wing, the middle third contains an entrance hall, a glazed court, and storerooms; the right third has offices and service rooms.*

and post-impressionist period in France.

The principal galleries are on the second floor and surround the court on all four sides (fig. 47). Most of them are two stories high (fig. 51). There are few openings either into the court or to the out-of-doors. Le Corbusier believed that the visitor's attention should be focused on the interior of the museum and on the works of art here displayed. Nonetheless, on each side of the building there is either a large window or a doorway (fig. 50). These are located so that they compensate for discontinuities in the overhead lighting system.

Architecturally, the galleries are by no means neutral. Close to each outside wall is a file of the

columns that support the building. Opposite is an almost unbroken series of what appear to be clerestory windows. In fact they are the sides of wide one-story ducts that virtually surround the central court and provide most of the light to the galleries. There is ample height to pass under the ducts into adjacent two-story spaces.

Since these light ducts are the "theme" of the Tokyo museum they must be described in some detail (fig. 52). They are corridors fifteen feet wide and twenty-one feet high, of which some nine and a half feet project above the roof and nine and a half feet hang down from the ceiling into the galleries. This leaves a space seven and a half feet high for the passage of visitors. A glance at the cross section shows that each duct occupies approximately a third of the width of each wing of galleries. Continuous windows line both sides of these ducts above and below the level of the roof, and there are frequent holes in their bottoms admitting light directly onto sculpture or flat cases placed beneath. Artificial lights are located at appropriate places to supplement or replace daylight. The roofs of the ducts are concave, giving them a hammocklike appearance when viewed from above. Le Corbusier took particular pride in the accessibility of all the lighting and the ease with which everything could be kept clean. American museum superintendents who have to struggle with the leaks inevitably generated by normal skylights may well envy the Japanese.

Such a detached description fails to suggest how unsatisfactory the painting galleries are. If one concentrates upon a single painting, one can see it well. But this takes an effort of will. The initial impression is of a needlessly complex corridor. The parade of columns dominates the row of small paintings; above all the contrast between the brightly lit and deeply dark surfaces is distracting (fig. 51).

Not quite all the galleries are two stories in height. Above the one-story galleries on the second floor of the museum are the minimum of offices that Le Corbusier provided for the director and the rest of the professional staff. The only elevator is for freight, but stairways abound, and being "frankly expressed" intrude upon the galleries like major pieces of bad sculpture (fig. 51).

47. *National Museum of Western Art. Plans of the first and second floors as executed.*

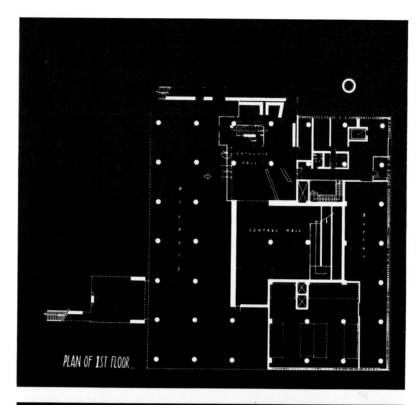

PLAN OF 1ST FLOOR

Buildings and Equipments

Compound area: 7.100 m²
Museum Building: Two storied building with a mezzanine, reinforced concrete, covering 4.180 m² area.
Floor surface of Exhibition Gallery: 4.180 m²
Equipments: Air-conditionning, Automatic regulation of Humidity.

_ PLAN OF 2ND FLOOR

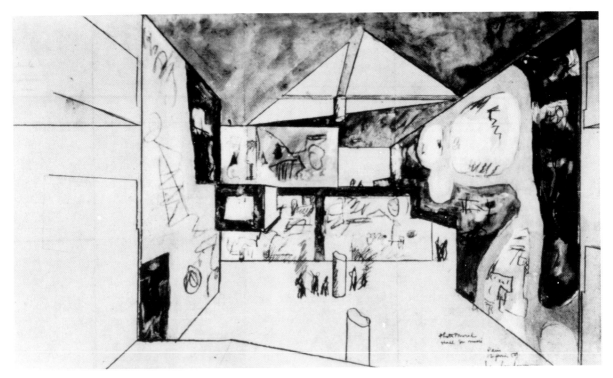

48. *National Museum of Western Art. Interior of the central court; all sculptures are by Rodin. Access is on the right. Looking out on the court are two semi-enclosed balconies for displaying small objects.*

49. *National Museum of Western Art. Le Corbusier's sketch of the central court with his proposed photo-murals. He seems to have envisioned few, if any, sculptures in this area.*

50. *National Museum of Western Art. Exterior, before the addition of the lecture hall wing.*

One of these gives access to the roof, an extraordinary plaza. In the center rises the immaculate triangular pyramid that skylights the court. Around it in a swastika-like arrangement are the comfortable tops of the four major light ducts, and surrounding the whole are twenty-four tidy garden beds that Le Corbusier intended to fill with flowers.

The exterior of the building consists of precast concrete panels which like the concrete trim are warm light gray in color (fig. 50). Pebbles were laid on the exposed sides of the panels to produce an admirably durable and stainproof surface. Though practical and long admired in France, many Anglo-Saxons are irrationally allergic to the appearance and feel of this composite surface.

All that now remains of Le Corbusier's projected esplanade is a bare square, little larger than the museum itself. This is at once defined by and isolated from the purlieus of adjacent cultural buildings by thin rows of trees or shrubs. Within the museum square, roughly opposite the two front corners of the building, are placed large casts of Rodin's *Burghers of Calais* and *Gates of Hell*, while in the corner next to the entrance is his *Thinker*. Of this aspect of their collective achievement Junzo Sakakura was especially proud. "In the end, it was possible at least to obtain a space for a small plaza where three of Rodin's best-known works could be displayed and thus to create a space wherein architecture and sculpture were harmoniously combined. I am happy that we were able in this way to add an element of clarity, of harmony, of quiet, and of strength to Le Corbusier's first building in Japan."[26]

The most important aspect of the National Museum of Western Art has been its success. Recently it has had to be greatly enlarged. The building has aroused little interest among architectural critics or Le Corbusier's biographers, perhaps because few of them have seen it, perhaps because it is only a fragment from an integrated plan, perhaps because of a natural tendency to avoid discussing those late works that were executed for the master rather than by him.

The standard comment on the National Museum of Western Art is that it is not one of Le Corbusier's best buildings. The museum professional will observe that the windows and doors, one of which the architect carefully arranged on each side of the second-floor galleries, have had to be closed and covered over, either because of excessive condensation or for reasons of security. Moreover, professional standards of climate control have advanced greatly in the last quarter century, and this building has proved exceptionally intractable.

The architectural historian will consider the building a compendium of ideas that were presented with greater conviction in earlier designs, for example the ramps. The major new contribution is the light ducts. Preoccupation with

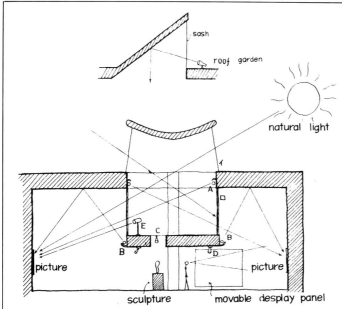

Lighting in the Nineteenth Century Hall
  Triangular skylight with glass on north side
  (in bad weather natural light can be aug-
  mented by fifteen 1-kilowatt projection lamps)

Lighting in Galleries
  ⌐. Heat-absorbent rough wire glass
  ⌐. Transparent or translucent sliding glass
     panels, roll blinds, for modulating light
  A. Supplementary 40 W fluorescent lamp
     (natural white)
  B. Same as A
  C. Spotlight (200 W with diffusing filter)
  D. Movable spotlight (sockets spaced every
     three meters) for use with movable dis-
     play panels
  E. Movable floor-spotlight for special effects

51. *National Museum of Western Art. Second-floor gallery. This photograph makes clear the small size of the paintings in relation to the gallery designed specifically for them. The clerestory dispenses adequate and admirably even light, but the contrast between light and dark spaces is at least as sharp as the photograph suggests.*

52. *National Museum of Western Art. Diagram showing lighting of central court and second-floor galleries.*

the optimum lighting of paintings was characteristic of the years right after the war, witness the remodeling of the Uffizi, the Huntington Galleries, and Wright's scheme for the Guggenheim. Characteristically, Le Corbusier's approach was abstract. Although this museum was designed for a specific collection, dominantly a group of relatively small paintings from one school, the architect's solution is designed for works of art of any size or period. In most of the galleries the paintings seem overwhelmed by the power of the building. In short, the Tokyo museum denigrates many of the individual works of art it displays without itself making an important architectural statement. The contrast with the Guggenheim is complete.

To such nay-saying some ordinary visitors may take strong exception. The most significant aspect of the Matsukata collection is the assemblage of bronzes by Rodin. The outstanding achievement of the National Museum of Western Art is the superb presentation it offers these works. They punctuate the broad space of the plaza. They establish a human scale and bring liveliness to the confusion of austere forms that is the present state of the court. They enrich the occasional small balcony galleries on the upper floor. The intensity of Rodin's individual statues, the diversity and range of his achievement make an impact at the National Museum of Western Art as they do in no other museum.

Walter Gropius and the Huntington Galleries

The Huntington Galleries, at Huntington, West Virginia, now called the Huntington Museum of Art, is an extraordinary institution.[27] Its development has been influenced by the fact that it is in a tri-state region where, within a radius of fifty miles, there is no other art institution, "no zoo, no planetarium, no aquarium, no natural history museum, no science museum, nor any historical museum." In response to public needs it has acquired a diversity of collections and places exceptional emphasis on differing temporary exhibitions and educational programs. These have "produced a proprietary response from a broad and varied audience which includes art lovers, craftspersons, bird-watchers, trail walkers, star gazers, music afficionados and theatregoers."[28] The Galleries include a substantial extension designed by Walter Gropius.

The Galleries' possessions now include oriental prayer rugs, "a renowned antique arms collection, a superb collection of Georgian silver in the company of English portraits," nonacademic American portraits, early pottery and furniture, a small but fine group of Barbizon paintings, and paintings by leading American artists of the late nineteenth and early twentieth centuries, as well as an extensive group of prints ranging from Albrecht Dürer to Jim Dine. The Galleries own an unusually attractive group of three-dimensional objects by sculptors from Daniel Chester French to George Rickey. In addition, because the making of glass is an important local industry, the museum has been acquir-

ing historic and contemporary works of art in that medium. Soon the museum will require the construction of a new gallery for the proper display of this collection.[29]

Most of the works of art in the Huntington Galleries are small, objects of a size that might be found in a collector's home. The collections are so extensive that the museum's policy is to exhibit them in a series of rotating temporary exhibitions.[30] Virtually the only possessions that are permanently on display are the collection of firearms and the largest sculptures, most of them medium-sized objects.

The Huntington Galleries was incorporated in 1947 by a group of local citizens. The central figure at the start seems to have been Herbert Fitzpatrick, a wealthy lawyer and a bachelor. He did not know what to do with his collection or with an estate he owned at the southern edge of the Huntington suburbs. He and his younger friend, David Fox, brought other men like themselves together and they resolved to establish a cultural institution. None of these individuals was exceedingly wealthy.[31] Fox lived near the Fitzpatrick estate, as perhaps did some of their associates. In any event the project was generally thought elitist; ultimately the location was widely criticized as being too far from the center of Huntington.[32]

In 1952 Fitzpatrick bequeathed to the Galleries his fifty-four-acre estate and his works of art. These were an appealing personal collection of fine small paintings by the French impressionists. In the same year the trustees erected a modest building designed by Small, Smith & Reeb of Cleveland on a hilltop plateau near the southeast corner of their property (fig. 53).

Initially the Galleries had only Fitzpatrick's works of art and a few

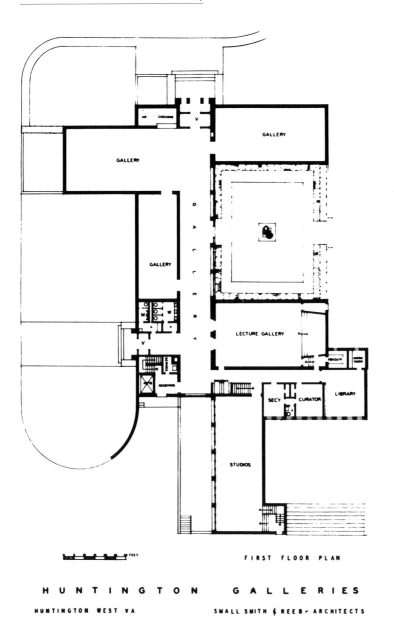

GALLERY

GALLERY

GALLERY

LECTURE GALLERY

SEC'Y   CURATOR   LIBRARY

STUDIOS

FIRST FLOOR PLAN

H U N T I N G T O N   G A L L E R I E S

HUNTINGTON WEST VA.   SMALL SMITH & REEB · ARCHITECTS

53. *Huntington Galleries, Huntington, West Virginia. Plan of the original building by Smith, Small & Reeb, 1952.*

other individual gifts of objects. They hoped the new building would encourage other gifts, and, indeed, works of art did begin to arrive, slowly at first, then almost too rapidly. Herman P. Dean presented a collection of firearms in 1952; Mrs. Arthur Spears Drayton the largest gift the museum has received, over three hundred works of American art.

Little information survives as to the original program for this building. Stripped-classic in style, it appears to have been a conventional small museum, though one terminal wing of the building contained studios and presumably was intended "for the study of arts and crafts by adults and children." Essentially it was a one-story building, in plan a letter T superimposed upon a letter F (shown upside down in fig. 53). At one end there was a piered entrance leading into the vertical element of this double letter, a central corridor with galleries opening off it, right and left. Although much of the corridor had glass from floor to ceiling, none of the side galleries had natural light. A second door was located directly opposite the mid-horizontal of the F, opening to a wing that contained a lecture gallery, administrative offices, and the service entrance. The far end of the vertical element of the F was two stories of studios. In plan the museum was a well-thought-out sequence of rooms, in elevation a sprawl of severe prisms with a single pompous element, the classically piered main entrance (fig. 57, right). What were either inadequate or lacking were rooms for adult activities related to art— a library, a lecture hall, and facilities for openings and other such public occasions.

In 1967 the Henry L. and Grace Doherty Charitable Foundation offered the trustees three quarters of a million dollars (later increased to a million) to expand the Huntington Galleries. One member of the board was accustomed to spending a winter vacation at an inn in Arizona. There she had made the acquaintance of Walter Gropius, who shared at least this facet of her taste in relaxation. So the building committee of the board turned to Gropius' firm, The Architects Collaborative, and asked if they would design an extension to the existing building. Gropius accepted with alacrity, choosing as his associate-in-charge Malcolm Ticknor. His was an unusual position, for while Gropius conceived buildings, he never drew them. The extension was completed in 1970.[33]

Gropius had long thought about the place art should occupy in life and had strong convictions as to the function and proper functioning of museums. He had even, so he said, designed an art museum. He had never built one. He had, however, published an essay that represents the clearest statement about the problem by any leading practitioner of the International Style; and the museum he eventually did build at Huntington can be more precisely related to its architect's ideals than can any other discussed in this book. In that essay Gropius had pointed to

the museum's visitor as the principal person to be served. . . . This will necessitate a study of the average visitor's psychological makeup, and I believe this to be even more important than the utilitarian aspects involved. . . .

It is a scientific fact that a human being needs frequently changing impressions in order to keep his receptivity in a state of alertness. . . . The capacity of a visitor to receive the messages of many masterpieces crowded together will dwindle rapidly unless we are able to refresh him frequently. His mind must be neutralized after each impression before a new impression can sink in. . . .

The exhibition spaces themselves, and the distribution of the exhibits in them should create a sequence of arresting surprises which must be well timed and properly scaled to fit the visitor's susceptibility. . . .

Today's democratic citizen will act with bored indifference to oversized spaces intended to impress him by mere bigness. . . . Man should be large in proportion to the architectural spaces. . . .

The various departments of the museum should be laid out as large, neutral spaces, enclosed by a permanent shell. . . . Rigidity of arrangements should be avoided for all departments. Doors from room section to room section should be avoided. This will create a desirable continuity of space which will keep the visitor inquisitive and expectant, and this is, after all, our foremost task.

The big problem of how to obtain proper lighting will give the museum program committee even greater headaches. . . . The best artificial light which tries to bring out all the advantages of an exhibit is, nevertheless, static. . . . Natural light, however, is dynamic, is alive as it changes continuously. The "fleeting occurrence" caused by the change of light is just what we desire. . . .

I have come to the conclusion that, for any exhibit . . . windows as a light source can still offer a legitimate solution. Not only will a glance through a window on the outside help to neutralize the visitor's mind and prepare him for new impressions, but a daylight window also offers the inestimable factor of change in illumination according to the change of weather. . . .

True architecture is the creation of new living space for man; its aim is to offer a "life in space" in full relationship with it, rather than a retreat from space in a fixed enclosure. . . .

We experience today a preference for transparency in buildings . . . to achieve a floating continuity of space. Space seems to move in and out of the building, and sections of the infinite outdoor space become a definite part of the architect's space composition, which does not stop at the enclosing exterior walls, but is carried beyond them into the open. . . .

Indoor and outdoor space together become one indivisible entity, both as an artistic composition and as a diversified receptacle of life.[34]

Although the above remarks concern the designing of museums in general, two omissions should be noted. Gropius concerns himself only with the passive visitor who goes to a museum to see what the staff has chosen to display. He is not concerned with any other kind of visitor, for example the patron who goes to an opening for the pleasure of the occasion or the visitor who has strong interests of his own and for whom the accessibility of works of art that are not on display may be of prime importance. Indeed nowhere does he mention the all-but-universal headache, adequate storage. Second, though few would deny that the museum visitor is the principal person to be served, museums are also designed for the safe care of valuable objects. Nowhere does Gropius concern himself with this issue, and the word "conservation" is not even implied.

When confronted with the specific problem of designing the Huntington Galleries Gropius introduced a further consideration, stressing "both the improvement of historic knowledge of art as well as the artistic creativity of the younger generation for the cultural benefit of the whole community."[35] He dealt with educational matters more precisely in a speech he gave at the ground breaking for the expansion. He seems to have been primarily concerned with children, although adult education must be a major preoccupation of any American art museum.

A society such as ours which has conferred equal privileges on everybody, will have to acknowledge its duty to activate the general responsiveness to spiritual and aesthetic values. . . . The only active influence which our society can take towards such a goal is to see to it that our educational system for the next generation will develop in each child, from the beginning, a perceptive awareness which intensifies his sense of form. He is born with eyes, but can he see? No, he has to learn to see. . . . Beauty is a basic requirement of life. When a society has recognized this and educated itself to "see," it will finally produce a cultural image.

I ask your permission to stress particularly the aspect of workshop education in the gallery, which is perhaps less obvious in its scope and value to the average person than appreciation of the past, but ever so much more important for the future generations' creative attitude.[36]

Such were the principles. They could hardly have been stated more clearly and forcibly. What is interesting is to see how Gropius compromised with them at Hun-

tington, in part because the existing building and financial stringency limited his ability to carry them out. More importantly, when it came to actual designing he was more interested in producing a building that would be satisfactory as a whole than in using his portion to demonstrate an immutable ideology.[37]

The chairman of the building committee and the board of trustees were by no means entirely clear or in complete agreement as to the museum's needs or their relative priority. However, a rough list of desiderata was drawn up and much time was spent with Gropius, balancing one demand against another. It seems clear that he skillfully guided the deliberations and that the final program in large part reflected his convictions. Throughout the entire process of creation, as the trustees still testify, he remained deeply, personally, and touchingly committed to this building. At the last he even insisted that a tree of his choice should be craned over the almost completed structure and planted in the center of the courtyard.

Gropius thought air conditioning an extravagance and would happily have dispensed with it, spending the money so saved to build additional space. He resented the small areas devoted to food preparation, remarking: "We are not in the eating business."[38] Today, one of the most keenly felt faults of the building is the inadequacy of the areas available for the preparation and serving of food. On two points his opinions were decisive. The enlargement, though not extravagant, must be well built.[39] The training of people in the making of art (children especially) was of primary importance. The existing training wing must be supplemented by a series of five studios. But the committee was equally determined. On no ac-

count must the cost of the building exceed the budget. A vision of five studios was fine, but they would build only as many as they could immediately afford. In the event this proved to be three.

A fundamental concern of Gropius was to take maximum advantage of the museum's admirable site. This dictated the expansion of the building toward the south where there were splendid views (fig. 54). Despite the generous acreage Mr. Fitzpatrick had presented, the flat hilltop site itself is restricted in size, being surrounded by steep slopes. Moreover, located as it is at the suburban limit, the normal access is by private car. Site planning for the extension involved a careful balance of three factors: desirable and likely attendance, parking space (figured at 2.2 persons per car), and the museum's need for more room. The balance struck between these factors seems to have been brilliantly successful.[40]

A second concern was to create a nature trail along the adjacent wooded slope. Gropius provided a sculpture terrace projecting from the southeast corner of the building. This was an admirable place to admire the view and also served as a start for the pathway. It was several years before funds became available for the woodland aspect of this project.

The main portion of the extension was a U-shaped unit attached to the F in such a way as to create an attractive court on two levels

54. *Huntington Galleries. Plan for the expanded building as proposed by Walter Gropius and The Architects Collaborative. In 1970 it was completed almost as shown. The extension occupies the right half of the drawing.*

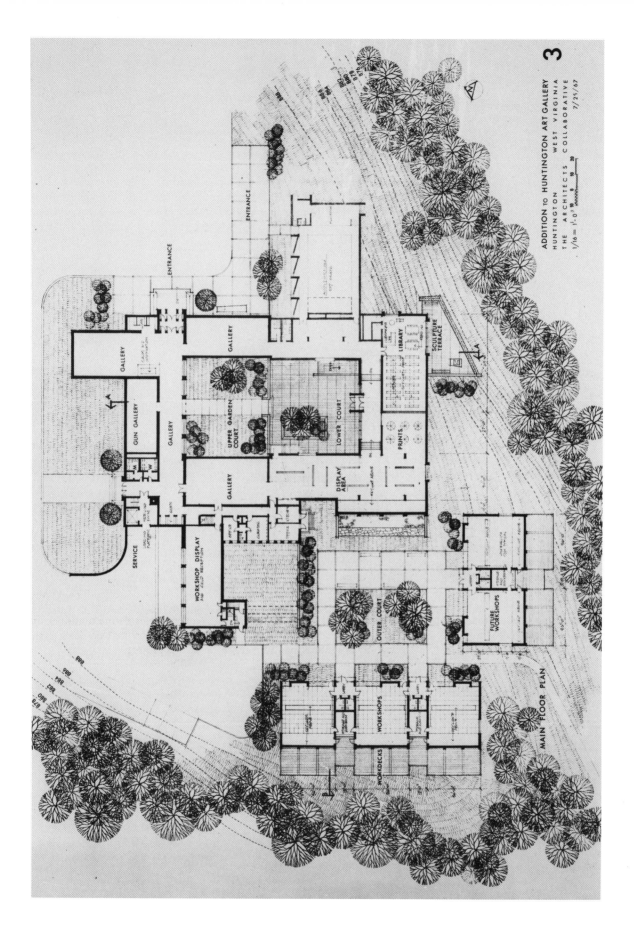

ADDITION to HUNTINGTON ART GALLERY
HUNTINGTON   WEST VIRGINIA
THE ARCHITECTS   COLLABORATIVE
1/16 = 1'-0"   7/25/67

3

MAIN FLOOR PLAN

55. *Huntington Galleries. Main courtyard. The original courtyard is slightly higher than the extension. At left is the stairway down to the sculpture terrace. On the roof at right are the clerestory windows and half-barrel vault that light Gropius' large display area.*

56. *Huntington Galleries. Architect's drawing of the workshop court as completed by Dean and Dean in 1976. At left is the half-barrel vault of the display area; at right, Gropius' studios. At center is the stage in front of Dean and Dean's modified studios.*

(fig. 55). In addition to providing an admirable space for the display of sculpture, this gave the plant a visual coherence it had hitherto lacked. Around the court were grouped a library and several galleries while projecting from it were two units of the original building as well as a new auditorium. The central court plays a predominant part in the building. One is conscious of it everywhere. Every gallery looks out upon it; even the supposedly enclosed print area has an inside window looking indirectly into the court.

The scale of the court is charming; the drop in level is attractive, creating only one difficulty, the necessity of introducing stairs rising from the southern into the eastern and western wings of the cloister. The steps descending into the passage leading down to the sculpture terrace are an attraction. Since the entrance from the court to the terrace runs under the library, this is supported by slablike piers. These appear elsewhere, within the building, and become a minor design motif (fig. 58).

Whether they were included in the original program or not, because of Gropius' primary concern with "workshop education" he proposed to create two rows of small studios on the west, thus forming a second, semi-enclosed court, "a workshop quadrangle" (fig. 56). One row of these studios was executed at that time; the other was built in 1976 by the local architectural firm of Dean and Dean. (The final studios differed in form from the others so that their inner walls could provide a stage at one end of the second courtyard.) Gropius' studios are singularly straightforward. They accomplish what is expected of them with admirable simplicity. Inside there is a strong contrast between the main part of the room, which has only side light, and the bright clerestory-lit rear wall.

Three considerations influenced Gropius' elevations. He imaginatively exploited the possibilities offered by the landscape, creating, for the views they provided, not only the projecting sculpture terrace without but large, carefully placed windows within (fig. 58).

Where the old and the new sections of the building joined he avoided a sharp contrast (figs. 55, 57). Both the extension and the original building were made of a beautiful pale orange brick, with a rather conspicuous masonry trim, light in color. In the original building the trim was gray limestone; in the addition it is an exposed concrete form. By taking great care, the builders were able to match the two trims in color. For acoustical reasons Gropius built the north side of the auditorium as a series of slightly diagonal brick panels. The piers that separate them ingeniously echo the similar forms of the original entrance, but lack its mini-post-office pomp.

At least implicitly Gropius condemned the interiors of normal art museums because he found them monotonous. He recommended variety. The original galleries had linoleum floors; these he left undisturbed, but provided the new galleries with wooden parquet. (The linoleum floors were later replaced with parquet also.)

Gropius favored natural lighting for the display of art; the original galleries had no natural light. This he left unchanged, but he painted both walls and ceilings white. In his own galleries the walls were covered with beige cloth to harmonize with his parquet floors. He introduced a variety of natural light and a diversity of ceiling treatments.

The relatively small, rectangular older galleries were ill-suited to the varying demands of those ambitious temporary exhibitions that constitute such an important part

of the Galleries' program. Hence Gropius provided a large, open display area with three narrow, slab-like piers as its only fixed internal elements (figs. 54, 58). Adjacent to this is a space with little natural light devoted to the display of prints. These are arranged in four print wheels, an astonishing resurrection of nineteenth-century museum practice. Beneath the L shape of these galleries, a generous though already insufficient basement space was set aside for storage of works of art.

Gropius' concern with the technology of display is manifest at Huntington in his frequent use of waffle-slab ceilings permitting easily movable and removable panels to break up the area beneath them. Also electric light can be plugged in almost anywhere. A particular feature of the display area, the auditorium foyer gallery, and the studios is the clerestory windows on top of a low section of wall facing half-barrel vaults.[41] These drench the wall opposite with reflected light (fig. 58). Effective inside, on the exterior such a protruding vault creates a form of startling ungainliness (fig. 56).

Perhaps the happiest example of what Gropius achieved is the suite of galleries running out from the original entrance hall on the east side of the main court. This is a pleasant area, conventionally lit by glass doors from floor to ceiling. First follows an original windowless gallery with doors in opposite corners and an ingenious coved ceiling that masks the ample artificial lighting. The auditorium foyer gallery, next, has a splendid window on the court, and opposite a clerestory throwing light on the rear wall of the auditorium. Between, a relatively narrow area of waffle-cove ceiling is supported by two slab piers. The vista from the reception desk continues across the end of the south cloister gallery, through the library door to a final

57. *Huntington Galleries. Entrance and auditorium wing.*

window with a view of the distant hills. It is a remarkable series of spaces, uniform in their almost domestic scale but varying in the degree and nature of their illumination and furnishing. Here, more overtly than in any other portion of the building, Gropius does "achieve a floating continuity of space," unifying indoors with two aspects of the outdoors.

The corresponding sequence on the west side of the court is less happy. The first gallery is the original lecture gallery, transformed. Perhaps just because it is such a large high room, handsome in its proportion, Gropius may have felt obliged to create a sizable contrasting display area beyond (fig. 58). Empty, this seems low, both too broad and too long for its height. To be sure, it was never intended to be seen when empty. Rather it was to be broken up by a varying arrangement of objects or panels. As already mentioned, the large waffle ceiling is supported by three slab piers. Two of these are placed so close to the edge of the clerestoried wall that they define a brilliantly lit corridor along that wall. This makes for too drastic a contrast with the adjacent darker area beneath the heavy waffle slab. Large though it is, the window on the court is still too small adequately to illumine this central area. Once again the vista from the entrance ends in a splendid window giving on to the view.

There were few criticisms of the Gropius extension by the staff. The restricted kitchen facilities have already been mentioned. A subtler point is the complete visual separation between the museum wings proper and the workshop quadrangle. A visitor coming to view the collections or a temporary exhibit would have no awareness of the existence of the studios. Yet these were the most unusual feature of the entire complex.[42]

One is recurrently aware of the friendly, enclosed central courtyard on the one hand and of the

58. *Huntington Galleries. Display area. Screens and lights can be placed almost anywhere. Right, the half-barrel vault spreads even light on paintings. There is a greater contrast of light and dark areas than this photograph suggests.*

surrounding beauty of the woods and the steeply sloping hills on the other. The clerestories provide ample, even, and varying light, the quantity easily controlled by vertical slats—vertical Venetian blinds in effect. Less satisfactory are the waffle-slab ceilings. Their very massiveness tends to crush the small works of art hung on the walls beneath. Individual bulbs in the apex of each domelet can focus admirably on single objects, but the effect on a stretch of wall surface as a whole is spotty. It is hard to believe this problem is insoluble.

As was mentioned earlier, most of the works of art in the permanent collections are small. These are generally displayed in happy groupings—a cluster of contemporary glass set on shelves against a huge window, or groups of American vernacular art in the narrow south cloister walk. The diversities in Gropius' domestic-scale interiors provide a desirable variety of opportunities to present these groupings appropriately. But this is at a cost. One remembers the admirable courtyard, the splendid lecture hall, and the enviable diversity of interiors. One hardly recalls a single Gropius gallery as an entity. Rather, the lasting image is of a compilation of ingenious, indeed gratifying solutions to individual problems.

In conclusion, one cannot but be struck by two phenomena. The first is that the Gropius extension to the Huntington Galleries exists. It is a prejudice of the more prosperous parts of this country that they alone have been the patrons of the high style in art. Happily this is not true, as proven, for example, by Frank Lloyd Wright's campus at Florida Southern College in Lakeland or by the extension of the Huntington Galleries. The fact is that the self-satisfied

residents of the prosperous parts of the country know too little about architecture elsewhere in the United States.

Secondly. Gropius' style did not evolve very much; moreover, his principles changed hardly at all. It is easy to assume that his buildings are as rigid as the image projected by his public personality. In fact, during the seventeen years since the Gropius extension was completed, the Huntington Galleries have grown extraordinarily and have evolved into a very different kind of institution. Yet the building he provided has proved exceptionally adaptable.

Gropius was without question the greatest teacher of the visual arts in the twentieth century. At the time of his selection he was considered, and probably considered himself, one of the greatest architects of our time. The extension of the Huntington Galleries is one of his most modest buildings. Modest not alone in size, but in the effort to make an adaptation to an undistinguished earlier structure the essence of his design. This involved a restraint in the expression of his personal style and a desire for coherence in the whole building that is unique in the design of art museums by leading architects of the twentieth century.

Such an attempt can involve losses; it can also produce gains. If his contribution to the Galleries is not a particularly vivid exposition of his architectural principles, it is also one of his most sympathetic buildings. It is warm in color because on the exterior he reproduced the singularly beautiful orange brick of the original. It is soft in texture because in deliberate contrast to the white plaster of the original galleries he chose a beige textile to cover the walls, and a parquet floor that relates pleasantly to them, both in color

and in texture.

The confusion of the original scheme he rectified by the creation, as his central feature, of a singularly attractive court. The demands of an exceptionally active program of temporary exhibitions he met by providing a diversity of spaces and a variety of possible lighting effects. Precisely because the original building was stamped by the would-be monumentality of its entrance, he sought a combination of intimacy and surprise. If this is not a great building, it is an enchanting one. It has the particular appeal that comes from the careful consideration of the desires and needs both of those who visit it and those who run it. Despite the implications of the entrance, the Huntington Galleries are no palace. Rather they exemplify the diverse casual charms of a manor house.

Mies van der Rohe in Berlin

The building of the Guggenheim was a private venture; the building of the Tokyo museum, though commissioned by the government, was an eccentric obligation gracefully fulfilled, but from the official point of view a minor matter. The new National Gallery in West Berlin, by contrast, is a major museum of modern art.[43]

In asking Ludwig Mies van der Rohe to design a new building for the city's collection, thoughtful members of the city government consciously turned to the man they considered most appropriate, not only because of his stature as an architect but also because of his deep association with Berlin. The invitation was submitted to Mies, then living in Chicago, in 1961 on his seventy-fifth birthday. He accepted on condition there should be no interference from the city's Department of Buildings.[44] This the city Senate achieved. Building began in the autumn of 1965 and was completed in September 1968. Mies, like Wright and Le Corbusier, never saw his completed building. Too ill to attend the opening, he died a few months later.

Mies' plans envisioned a very expensive building. Rather than reduce his proposal, the city sought other sources of support. Berlin's collection of modern art had come into being immediately after the second World War. This collection was now merged with the possessions of the former National Gallery (a collection of nineteenth- and twentieth-century art that had belonged to the Prussian state and was now administered by a foundation). The whole was then housed in the new National Gallery, to which the Federal Republic, as well as the governments of the ten West German states, contribute funding.[45] The merger meant more objects to care for, but the building provided for them was no larger. Once again architectural beauty had triumphed over adequate storage.

South of Berlin's Tiergarten, between Kemperplatz and the Landwehrkanal, was an area almost wholly devastated during the war. Indeed the only structure of consequence to survive was the Matthäikirche, an 1864 quasi-romanesque building designed by the local architect Friedrich August Stüler (figs. 62, 63). On these empty acres the city government had decided to create a cultural center. Only a couple of blocks from the East German wall, it would be not too far from the middle of town if Berlin were ever reunited. The center was to include among other buildings a concert hall, a public library, and five additional museums.[46] A prime site on the canal, across the street from the huge new public library, was set aside for the new National Gallery.

Mies proposed a sizable underground museum opening at the back onto a sculpture garden (figs. 59, 61). This was to house every activity of the institution except temporary exhibitions. For these a huge pavilion was provided at ground level, on top of the museum proper (fig. 62). Both portions are square in plan, the lower one supported by columns spaced twenty-two feet apart (as against twenty-three apart in Le Corbusier's museum in Tokyo). The underground museum, with twelve bays each way, is thus virtually twice the length (or four times the area) of Le Corbusier's museum. The pavilion above has seven bays. Below, the ceiling heights in Berlin are fourteen feet; above, twenty-eight feet.

Of the lower floor little need be said. At the very rear is a parking lot for eighty cars, while along the left side a ramp for trucks descends to the shipping entrance. The director's and the conservation office face the submerged sculpture garden; from all the other offices one gets intimate views of the ramp. The entry stairs down from the pavilion debouch into a vacant-seeming central hall (fig. 60), a rather too ample point of departure for visits to the bathroom, the shop, the administrative offices, the restaurant, or the galleries. All are separated by substantial partitions. They define spaces varied in shape and uniformly beautiful in proportion. Obviously Mies and many people do not share Frank Lloyd Wright's belief that art looks best in naturally changing daylight. Almost all the lower galleries in the National Gallery are literally in the cellar and artificially lit; one never escapes a depressing awareness of these facts. The lighting, designed by the museum staff, is excellent. The galleries at the back have a row of piers a short distance behind glass walls. The latter run from floor to ceiling and open onto the sculpture garden. These galleries are among the most beautiful spaces created in the twentieth century (fig. 61).

The sculpture garden is also beautiful, enlivened on one side by the lively rear elevation of the museum and opposite by a long pool. As yet the pieces on display are conventional and too familiar, for example Renoir's *Washerwoman*. But Mies loved figures such as this; they appear again and again in his architectural renderings. Far more appealing are the large Calder stabile and the ample bronze by Henry Moore at the rear corners of the granite platform, overlooking the garden. Brilliantly placed, they conduct simultaneous dialogues

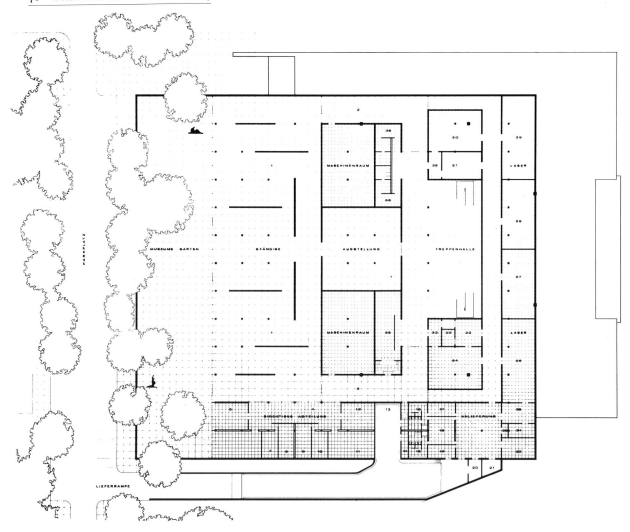

59. *New National Gallery, West Berlin, completed 1969; architect Ludwig Mies van der Rohe. Plan of the lower floor. Large squares indicate the floor of galleries and related areas; the stair hall is at right. Small squares indicate offices, storage, and other service functions. The bases of the eight piers supporting the roof of the pavilion appear on this plan as large black dots; the smaller dots represent the many slender columns that support the plaza above the lower floor.*

60. *New National Gallery. Stair hall, lower floor. This is the traffic center, giving access to the permanent collections, rest rooms, shop, and offices. It is likely to contain relatively little art and relatively many people.*

with one another, with the upper portion of the museum, and with the adjacent Matthäikirche (fig. 63).

Architecturally, the pavilion is the climax of the new National Gallery. It rises from a large granite platform, partly the roof of the museum, partly the leveled top of a low hill (fig. 62). The standard cliche is to compare the platform and the pavilion to the Acropolis and the Parthenon, and indeed the granite platform is a modest Acropolis. It sets the pavilion apart from the nearby world of cars, buses, trucks, and pedestrians, the world of people too busy to look at works of art.

The pavilion consists of a square steel roof, six feet deep, supported on eight steel piers each some three feet across. These are at the edge of the roof, arranged in pairs in such a way that the corners of the roof are cantilevered. Set some twenty-five feet back from the edge of the roof are four glass walls that create the pavilion proper. Revolving doors on the side toward the Potsdamerstrasse provide for entrance and exit. The granite base is a warm light gray; piers and roof

are black; the continuous curtain behind the glass is off-white from inside, warm neutral from outside.

Gropius, Wright, and Le Corbusier concerned themselves with the technology of lighting pictures, which Mies in the end relegated to the professional staff. He, however, was structurally adventuresome. The huge roof could only be designed using computers. To achieve the appearance of horizontality, allowance had to be made for the natural sag between piers and the tendency of the corners to drop. "Large segments of the roof structure were brought to the site and welded together on the ground. The columns were connected in a horizontal position by means of pin joints. The twelve hundred and fifty ton roof was then raised by hydraulic jacks to a position slightly above its final elevation . . . in approximately nine hours. The columns gradually swung into a vertical position during the lifting process. The entire structure was then slowly lowered into place."[47]

Within, the space is completely unbroken (fig. 64). Right and left, stairs of the utmost simplicity lead

to the museum below. Behind each is the plainest of enclosed wooden coat racks—oak wardrobes as it were. Toward the rear of the space are two piers veneered with green marble. Each of these contains a series of ducts, notably those that drain rain water from the roof.

Mies was an architect of comparatively few concepts. He declared: "I refuse to invent a new architecture every Monday morning. The Greeks took hundreds of years to develop the Doric column, but it worked. I do not wish to be interesting, I want to be right."[48] Throughout his career he had concerned himself with low buildings. Many were but a single story, though they served a surprising variety of functions—domestic, commercial, cultural. The pavilion of the new National Gallery represents the culmination of this aspect of his achievement as an architect.

The pavilion was the culmination, too, of Mies' concern with the proper display of works of art. James Johnson Sweeney recalled that Mies van der Rohe would often visit the Nierendorf Gallery in

New York. "He and his friend Karl Nierendorf used to take advantage of the weekend to clear the gallery walls of what was on view and amuse themselves in arranging a special collection of whatever they liked or wanted to see together from Nierendorf's stock. It might be . . . a single picture on an otherwise empty wall, [a mode of presentation] which so much appealed to Mies."[49] A collector himself, Mies had been concerned throughout his professional life with the presentation of works of art. Many of his extraordinary drawings, faint, suggestive, and almost irreproducible, give vivid testimony to this concern. To mention but three of many earlier projects: in 1912 he had designed a house in Berlin for the art collector Kroller; in 1928–29 he created the museumlike German pavilion at the Barcelona International Exposition; in the early 1940s *Architectural Forum* commissioned him "to produce a project appropriate to a

city of the future." Out of an infinitude of possibilities for this commission, his choice was a "museum for a small city" (fig. 65).

Compared to Wright or Le Corbusier, Mies was a man of almost no words. His preferred form of communication seems to have been aphorisms. Only when discussing the museum for a small city did he reveal many of his concepts concerning what these institutions should be. He wrote:

The museum for the small city should not emulate its metropolitan counterparts. The value of such a museum depends upon the quality of its works of art and the manner in which they are exhibited.

The first problem is to establish the museum as a center for the enjoyment, not the interment of art. In this project the barrier between the art work and the living community is erased by a garden approach for the dis-

61. *New National Gallery. Galleries facing the garden, lower floor. Since the ceiling is supported by columns, the partitions can be moved; this happens rarely.*

62. *New National Gallery. Plaza and pavilion, with the 1864 Matthäikirche and the new Philharmonic Hall in the background (rear left). Such was the site Mies was allotted that he could achieve the isolation he believed appropriate to a museum. Below the church can be seen the sculpture garden and lower-floor windows opening onto it.*

63. *New National Gallery. Pavilion, church, and Calder stabile.*

play of sculpture. Interior sculptures enjoy an equal spatial freedom, because the open plan permits them to be seen against the surrounding hills. The architectural space, thus achieved, becomes a defining rather than a confining space. A work such as Picasso's Guernica has been difficult to place in the usual museum gallery. Here it can be shown to greatest advantage and become an element in space against a changing background.

The building, conceived as one large area, allows every flexibility in use. The structural type permitting this is the steel frame. This construction permits the erection of a building with only three basic elements—a floor slab, columns and a roof plate. The floor and paved terraces would be of stone.

Under the same roof, but separated from the exhibit space would be the offices of administration. These would have their own toilet and storage facilities in a basement under the office area.

Small pictures would be exhibited on free-standing walls. The entire building space would be available for larger groups, encouraging a more representative use of the museum than is customary today, and creating a noble background for the civic and cultural life of the whole community.[50]

In contrast to the pavilion in Berlin, the ceiling of this museum is supported by rows of columns, four of which have been omitted to keep the sight lines in the auditorium clear. The roof above is supported by deep trusses, from which the ceiling hangs as well. Here is the germ of the spatial arrangement of the Berlin pavilion.

Notable, too, in the museum for a small city is how little space is devoted to special exhibits. In all the many Mies projects where architecture enframes works of art, the implication is that the installation is permanent. Ironically, Mies does not seem to have given much thought to the particular problems of temporary exhibitions.

When one turns from his writings to his drawings one notes his preference for large works of representational contemporary art. Each object is placed individually with a great volume of space separating it from the next object. He had a particular appreciation for the sculpture of Kolbe, Lehmbruck, Maillol, and Renoir. He delighted to imagine how their intensely modeled forms would look against the immaculate, luxurious planes of his buildings, against sheets of water or glass, against slabs of highly polished marble. In short, he was more sensitive to sculpture than any other major twentieth-century architect has been. His feeling for painting may have been less varied and less sure. In several designs an unframed Guernica rises like a screen from the floor. It is fair to say he often proposed to relate such imposing paintings to the natural background behind, be it water, leaves, or hills.

In the building of the National Gallery Mies held rigidly to the concept of the upper pavilion and would listen to no major suggested changes. Otherwise he talked at length to the museum staff about details of the design and was most accommodating in accepting their proposals and fulfilling their wishes. Despite his preference for large works, the inaugural exhibition was devoted to paintings by Mondrian (fig. 64).[51] The staff settled for white rectangular hanging screens to which the exhibits were attached. This arrangement obtained until the late seventies when it was abandoned because the screens were considered aesthetically insufficient for exhibiting paintings. Now, though dispositions vary from show to show, works of art are in general hung against or placed before solid panels a couple of feet thick. These are not necessarily unsatisfactory as backgrounds for individual works of art, but collectively they clutter up a great interior. One feels that a noble space, intended for some high purpose, has been adapted to some intensely communicative activity.

The basic problems of the Berlin pavilion are two. Mies' design was for masterpieces, isolated from one another. There is but one Guernica and it is not and is never likely to be in the new National Gallery. Indeed the pavilion is not even used for the modern masterpieces Berlin owns, but for temporary exhibitions.[52] In practice these are crowded with works of moderate size, often of the greatest interest; but rarely do such exhibitions contain nothing except masterpieces. A building that "allows every flexibility in use" is not likely to adapt perfectly to any one use. The noble space Mies conceived is visually ill-adapted to the functions it is currently expected to perform.

Most contemporary art is created for rooms of moderate height. As one remembers exhibitions in the new National Gallery and examines photographs of others there seems to be a disjunction of scale between the works of art and the space itself. If the objects and the panels against which they are hung clutter the space, the space, sometimes, overwhelms the objects. Of this possibility Mies was conscious. "It is such a huge hall," he declared, "that of course it means great difficulties for the exhibiting of art. I am fully aware of that. But it has such potential that I simply cannot take those difficulties into account."[53]

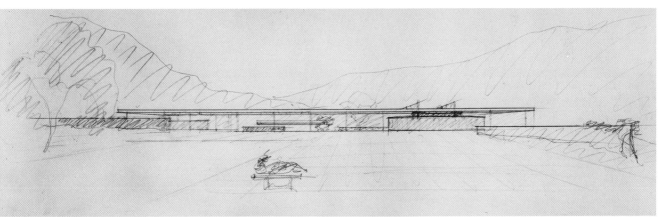

64. *New National Gallery. The opening exhibition, "Piet Mondrian." Though Mies regretted this choice of subject for that occasion, the installation suited his intentions. (The vertical mass in the background is a box containing ducts and pipes, sheathed in green marble.)*

65. *Mies van der Rohe, project, Museum for a Small City, c. 1942.*

But noble spaces are works of art in themselves, and are rare, perhaps especially rare in the twentieth century. We must be grateful to the city of Berlin, to the participating German governments, and to Mies.

In the case of most private collections that have generated public museums the architecture was determined by the collector's view of how the museum was to be experienced. In the four museums just discussed the forces that determined the design were more complex. Except for the seemingly passive Mr. Guggenheim, there were no collectors to be considered, nor were the professional staff of any of the museums able to mold the architecture entirely to suit themselves. On the other hand the architects were confused by objectives they were unable to bring into a single focus. They genuinely, if sentimentally, wished to serve "the public"; sentimentally because concerning the likely body of visitors they knew little that was specific and had no serious intention of finding out more. They all had strong convictions as to how objects should appear, but they deliberately ignored the kinds of art that would be shown in the buildings they were designing. Tokyo suits large bronze sculpture admirably, but the galleries are designed for collections in general, any collections, not for the French painting of a limited period that they were to contain. The same objection might be made of Huntington, although less justifiably, for that collection would change. Wright had a remarkable collection to house, important precisely because of the opportunities it presented for grouping or contrasting objects. He created a building

avowedly designed for the perfect display of single works of art. Mies designed for isolated masterpieces, though the pavilion was to be used for temporary exhibitions.

At Huntington and Tokyo the scale was too limited to achieve great architecture. The architects became interested in technical solutions, perhaps to hold in store until some large opportunity presented itself. The Guggenheim and the new National Gallery are among the unforgettable interiors of our century, but the art they contain is distracting. One vaguely hopes that someday they will cease to be museums and will be devoted to some alternative noble function that less disrupts their beauty.

·III·

When the Architect and the Professional Staff Collaborate

The Museum of Modern Art in New York

Compared to Gropius' Huntington Galleries, Le Corbusier's museum in Tokyo represented a compromise with the International Style; however pure formally, there was no thought of putting across a social message. The museum was simply a building appropriate to the display of nineteenth- and twentieth-century French art. That compromise between the social ideals of the International Style and the normal practice of art museums had been made long before, perhaps as early as anywhere at the Museum of Modern Art in New York, built in the middle 1930s.

Considered in detail, the history of this museum is extraordinarily complicated.[1] What follows is a simplified story, but accurate as regards the fundamentals. The museum opened in the autumn of 1929, renting quarters in a business building at 730 Fifth Avenue. A few months later, in May 1930, the museum's trustees got in touch with the firm of Howe and Lescaze and asked them to prepare designs for a new building, even though they had no definite site in mind. By the autumn of 1931 the architects had produced half a dozen designs in succession. Then matters came to a stop.[2] In April 1932 the museum moved to 11 East 53rd Street, a private house that was leased from John D. Rockefeller, Jr.[3] By 1936 the museum had outgrown these quarters and the trustees decided to build a new museum. They acquired the house they had been occupying and others on either side to achieve a piece of property 100 feet deep and 129 feet long on 53rd Street.

Later, partly by purchase and partly by gift, the museum acquired further adjoining property on East 54th Street that had also belonged to the Rockefellers, so that the museum and its garden are 200 feet deep, occupying a piece of land extending from their building on 53rd Street back to 54th Street.

The museum was unusual in many respects. The historical and geographical range of its interests was limited—western art from Cézanne and his contemporaries to the most advanced experiments of the present day. Its mission was "encouraging and developing the study of modern arts and the application of such arts to manufactures and practical life and the furnishing of popular instruction."[4] In 1936, when plans for the new building were being made, the museum's own collections were comparatively small. So the mission was being accomplished primarily by loan exhibitions, each of which lasted only a few weeks. But the typological range of the museum's interests was broad, involving, in addition to the traditional fine arts, photography, film, industrial design, and the dance.

Although from the start the museum charged admission and had attracted a large attendance, activities were made possible by the committed support of some twenty to thirty wealthy men and women. Thus individual trustees and especially the officers of the board were exceptionally closely involved in major operating decisions. In addition, partly to include a younger generation of enthusiasts, partly because of the diversity of areas in which the museum was interested, an exceptional number of advisory or supervisory committees were created.

These facts had several significant effects on the program for the new building. In most American art museums two thirds or more of the space is devoted to galleries. Initially in the Museum of Modern Art the proportion was to be only about one third. There were more curators than there were guards; indeed, if one includes the assistant curators, secretaries, and administrative staff, there were far more white collar than blue collar employees.[5] Provision had to be made for a large public to move easily through the galleries. From the start the freight elevator was also intended to transport visitors during popular exhibitions. Finally, a significant portion of the building would have to be allocated to the convenience and comfort of those patrons who supported the institution as well as the independent professionals who advised its staff.

The solution found was an eight-story building (fig. 66). The subbasement accommodated a film theater with lounge and some workshops; the basement, storage and rooms for preparing exhibitions; the ground floor a lobby with a bookshop, two galleries, and the loading dock (fig. 67). Above there were two floors of galleries (figs. 69, 70) and two of offices, and, finally, attractive roof terraces framing meeting rooms for members and trustees (fig. 72), as well as a kitchen.[6]

One final consideration affected the 53rd Street elevation. In the middle of Rockefeller Center there is a short street running parallel to Fifth Avenue. At one time it was proposed to continue this north to

66. *Museum of Modern Art, New York, completed 1939; architects Philip Goodwin and Edward Stone. Facade.*

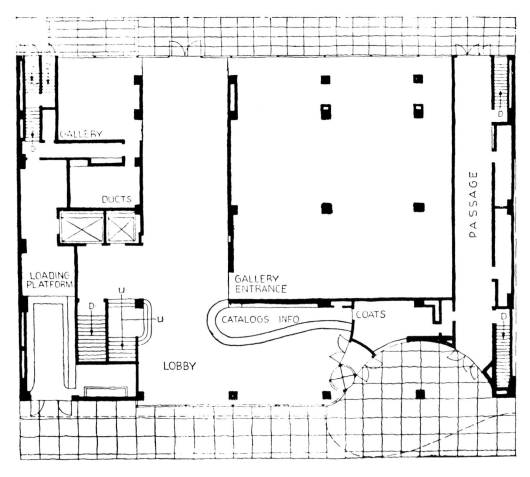

67. *Museum of Modern Art. Plan of the ground floor. The building is supported by a series of columns that define the whole as four bays by five. The spacing of bays is somewhat unequal, the westernmost (left-hand) row being wider than the rest to accommodate delivery trucks, the northernmost somewhat narrower to allow for skylighting the sculpture galleries on the third floor without unduly narrowing the building on the three floors above.*

68. *Museum of Modern Art. View from the lobby into the garden. Virtually the entire rear wall was glass from floor to ceiling to unite the interior with the garden.*

In the plan: GALLERY · DUCTS · LOADING PLATFORM · LOBBY · GALLERY ENTRANCE · CATALOGS INFO · COATS · PASSAGE

53rd Street. The Museum of Modern Art was to form a terminal visual accent to the extended street. Nelson Rockefeller, a member of the building committee and second president of the museum, was confident this street would be extended.[7] The design of the museum's facade must be considered with this confidence in mind (fig. 66).

The choice of an architect of any institution profoundly concerned with contemporary architecture poses a difficult problem. The Museum of Modern Art began by forming a building committee of three trustees. Director Alfred Barr, while in Europe arranging loans for an exhibition, was allowed to talk to three European architects about the commission. Only one of them, Mies van der Rohe, was interested, though he was immensely. Meanwhile the building committee talked to Philip Goodwin, a collector, a trustee, and the only architect on the board. He proved so wise that the board appointed him as architect with Edward Stone, a young designer, as his partner. Alfred Barr was not consulted and thereafter refused to meet with the building committee, but, in Stone's words, "was calling the shots from behind the scenes."[8] Barr was fired as Director but as Director of Painting and Sculpture he continued to be the dominating figure at the museum until his retirement.

The museum as originally built had three characteristics whose influence was enduring. The ground floor was a unity of galleries and garden (figs. 67, 68). Perhaps from the start, and certainly from early years, the garden was conceived as a gallery for the display of sculpture. It was undoubtedly the first public sculpture gallery in any city in the country. Philip Johnson, a

trustee, has on several occasions arranged the display of sculpture in this garden. There has always been a certain spatial conflict since the galleries formed a necklace of discrete rectangular spaces, whereas the garden is a single east-west entity (fig. 68). Doubtless this conflict could have been diminished had the architects known when they made their plans how extensive that garden was going to become. Barr believed passionately that works of art should be seen in daylight. On the two gallery floors of the museum (the second and the third), the entire south wall is of Thermolux (fig. 66). At that time this was a new material, chosen in order to diffuse the daylight. As originally built, these windows transmitted far too much daylight, and a false wall had to be constructed behind the Thermolux. On the north side, the three upper floors of the museum are cut back so that the third-floor galleries on this side can be skylit (fig. 71). They proved among the most satisfactory galleries anywhere for the display of sculpture.

The sculpture galleries are separated from the remainder of the third floor by a solid wall (fig. 69). Otherwise the second and third floors have no fixed partitions, only a dozen piers supporting the remainder of the building. Temporary screens can be arranged in any way the staff believes appropriate to the works of art being exhibited. The gallery floors of the Museum of Modern Art were the first in any major museum to be conceived like those of a warehouse, completely adjustable (fig. 70).

Aesthetically the building has many virtues—refined proportions, elegance in the choice and use of materials, an appealing and imaginative entrance (figs. 66, 67). It suffers inescapably on the 53rd Street facade from the fact that the

vocabulary of the International Style was developed for freestanding buildings, and this is all but two-dimensional. However, the architects did their ingenious best to mitigate the problem, by splendid lettering on the projecting east corner, by the glimpse of a roof slab protecting the terrace, and by the imaginative and "audacious sloped entrance."[9]

Within, the lobby area is humane in scale and informal, the garden provides a startling sense of escape, and nothing obtrudes upon the works of art. It is these one vividly remembers, not the envelope in which they were displayed.

The achievement of the Museum of Modern Art has been the most remarkable among art museums during the twentieth century. Starting in every respect from scratch, it has created widespread public awareness and understanding of a field of endeavor that in 1930 only a handful of experts took seriously. It has established the dominant set of standards in this field. It has assembled the outstanding collection of works of twentieth-century art, exceeding in many areas the best that can be found in the country of origin of the artists concerned. Its building has suited this achievement to perfection. When it was new and the institution young, it called attention to the museum's importance by its own novelty and distinction. It was practical at the start, and as the museum has grown and its needs have changed, it has proved eminently adaptable. As its novelty has worn off, it has come to be seen as a benevolently neutral background for the museum's brilliant and varied activities. Certainly, it has not for decades been considered in itself as a remarkable work of art; so it has not competed for attention with the works of art it contained. In all these respects

70

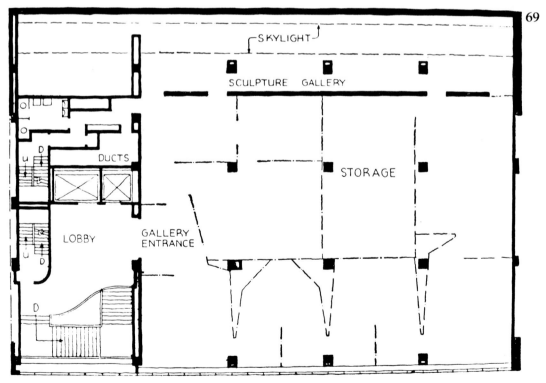

69

71

69. *Museum of Modern Art.
Plan of the third floor.*

70. *Museum of Modern Art.
Second-floor painting galleries, showing temporary partitions and adjustable spaces.*

71. *Museum of Modern Art.
Sculpture galleries, third floor; skylighting on statues by Lehmbruck.*

72. *Museum of Modern Art. Members' Room. The museum was dependent from the start on a considerable number of trustees, patrons, and advisers; the top floor made their visits and meetings enjoyable. Furniture was the best and latest.*

it may be considered architecturally the ideal museum. In several of them it contrasts strongly with more recent museum buildings.

Sadly, the Museum of Modern Art was among the first American art museums to face grave financial difficulties. It is said that the institution ran a deficit of a million dollars a year for a considerable number of years. American art museums have only four sources of support: income from endowment; memberships or other annual gifts; earnings (whether from fees paid at the entrance, from books and meals sold, or from the parking lot); and public subsidies (that is money from taxes), money given because a museum's existence is acknowledged to be a good thing, just as a public library is accepted as a good thing. In the fifties and sixties it became evident that for many museums all these sources were proving inadequate. The justification for support from taxes was the amount of service that could be provided, and this could most easily be measured by counting the number of visitors. If a million came, good. If two million came, that was twice as good and a museum had enhanced its chances of being subsidized. So some museums became concerned with the accommodation of truly enormous numbers of people and built extensions with that in mind.

Conspicuous among these was the Museum of Modern Art. Its success was phenomenal; to accommodate increasing activities and numbers of visitors it sprouted wings along 53rd Street, and taking over the building of the Whitney Museum it acquired an off-center tail leading back to 54th Street beside the west end of the garden. Yet by the late seventies it was still too small to meet demands. A daring extension was seen as a way to resolve both the problems of space and funds. Com-

plete reconstruction and the addition of yet another wing running north-south at the east end of the garden would accommodate the needed additional office space and increase the 40,500 square feet of galleries to 87,000. Sacrifice of some air rights along 53rd Street to accommodate a tower containing 263 rented apartments would provide additional funds.

Architecturally, the 1984 result was a masterpiece of understatement. Outside, the original white facade survives intact, contrasting sharply with the deliberately unassertive new construction. Asked how they liked the tower, early visitors replied: "What tower?" Inside, as Cesar Pelli, the architect of the extension, stated, the "rooms remain basically apartment-size." The only conspicuous addition is a five-story out-of-scale greenhouse that intrudes itself between the museum and the garden and encloses a double escalator. Rather conventional galleries impressively present the extraordinary permanent collection of twentieth-century art that Alfred Barr assembled. It is no longer a building one remembers, rather a commonwealth of display areas united by an escalator.[10]

The East Wing of the National Gallery, Washington

Perhaps the most prominent extension of an American art museum is the East Wing of the National Gallery of Art in Washington. Andrew Mellon, donor of the Gallery, had been forethoughtful. When, in the mid-1930s, he proposed to build a National Gallery in Washington he asked Congress not only to provide an adequate site, but also to set aside additional space for future expansion. He was alloted the three blocks between Constitution Avenue and the Mall, extending from Fourth to Seventh Streets. Here the original National Gallery was built (fig. 73). An additional block, adjacent to the east, between Third (alias Ceremonial Drive) and Fourth was reserved.[11] Any extension would presumably be placed in that area.

By the mid-1960s the National Gallery, as shaped by David Finley and John Walker, its first two directors, embraced three activities: acquiring works of art, presenting these to the public, and the scholarly study of art as well as the training of younger scholars.[12] The original building had made almost no provision for this third function and at this time the trustees decided to build a study center on the eastern block. I. M. Pei was consulted; he declared the available site too large and too important for a building that would only require a limited amount of space.[13]

Meanwhile the collections had increased more rapidly than originally expected, and the institution needed not only additional galler-

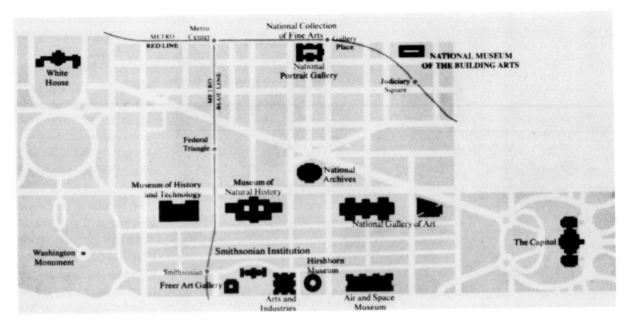

73. *Washington, D.C. Site plan from the Capitol to the Washington Monument, 1979. In this area, besides these public buildings, there are many government office buildings, almost all classical in style.*

ies but also storage space for works of art (almost wholly lacking in the original building).[14] Temporary exhibitions had come to play a far more important role than was originally envisioned, so space for receiving, uncrating, and shipping works of art was needed. In addition even existing attendance required a much larger restaurant and bookstore. All these considerations generated a demand for more offices. So the trustees asked Pei to design a new building to meet these needs; the resulting project eventually added approximately 600,000 square feet to the existing structure and almost doubled the amount of gallery space.[15] One function of these additional galleries was to house the museum's collection of twentieth-century art. Pei was asked to follow the program worked out by the staff and to build in harmony with

the original structure. The trustees said nothing about budget.

Pei set himself two challenges: "to design a building suitable to Washington's monumentality, without sacrificing human scale," and to create "a museum that has spatial excitement for visitors, but not at the expense of the exhibits."[16]

The site was a trapezoid with two right angles. Pei discarded the extreme eastern end, declaring it to be too narrow to be used effectively. He proposed a large basement, stretching from the old to the new building (fig. 74), treated at ground level as a plaza with a central fountain. The main new block would be trapezoidal, its faces running parallel to the streets. But he divided this block by a diagonal wall that created two unequal triangles, an isosceles triangle on Fourth Street and Pennangle on Fourth Street and Penn-

sylvania Avenue, and a smaller right triangle on the Mall and Third Street.[17]

He proposed to devote the cellar under the plaza to the servicing of people and objects. He provided a restaurant seating seven hundred and a large bookstore. The remaining space on this level and the whole sub-basement beneath serve for receiving works of art arriving by truck, handling them, and storing them, as well as for mechanical services. The large isosceles triangle was given over to the viewing of works of art, the smaller right triangle to the study center and to offices for the staff.

Functionally it was a brilliant solution and offered many unusual aesthetic possibilities of which Pei took full advantage. Thus water from the fountain in the plaza above is carried into the cellar as a cascade, which forms one wall of

the restaurant. Running east from
the northeast corner of the restaurant there is a diagonal corridor
172 feet long filled with two moving walkways. They connect the
basement facilities with the southwest corner of the new wing and
are convenient for those who wish
to go from one wing to the other.
Behind this corridor and the cascade, along the north side of the
basement, is the space for mechanical equipment and areas devoted to receiving, handling, and
storing works of art.

Above ground the East Wing is
two independent buildings that are
closely integrated (fig. 75). Each
has two facades and a prow where
it adjoins the other. The study
center is a form apart, sharing visually with the museum only a
clearly demarked portion of the
entrance porch. Essentially this
building is a covered court surrounded by seven stories of library
stacks and offices.[18] The museum is
a triangular block with towers at
its three corners. On the Fourth
Street facade a long open porch
connects two of the towers (fig.
76). Along Pennsylvania Avenue a

74. *National Gallery of Art,
Washington; John Russell Pope,
1941, and I. M. Pei, 1978. Basement plan. Everything in the upper
half was designed by Pei, including
the bookstore, the dining area, a diagonal moving walkway, lobbies, lecture halls, and temporary exhibition
galleries.*

75. *National Gallery of Art. Plan
of the main floor. In the East Wing,
above, the larger triangular museum
is clearly divided from the smaller triangular study and office building. Clear
also are the central glazed courts and
the connected diamond-shaped towers. All peripheral galleries can be
divided by flexible partitions.*

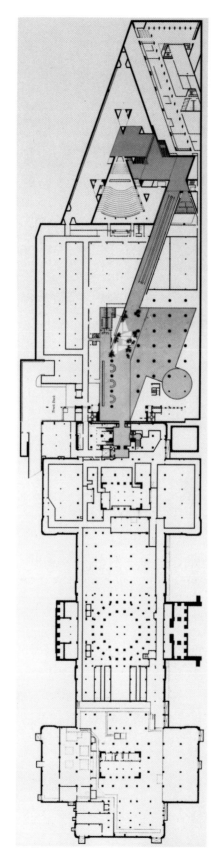

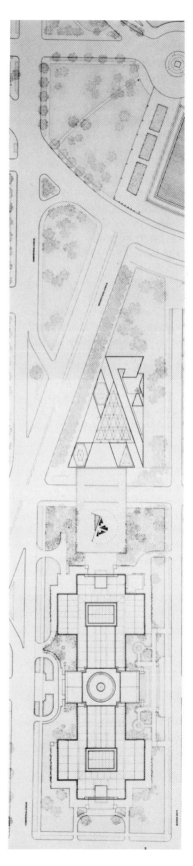

great recessed window performs the same function. Inside, this building too is arranged around a large, covered court.

Coming from the West Wing and the basement restaurant, the moving corridor terminates at a splendid tapestry; to the north of this is a lobby (fig. 74). At one side of the lobby are the main stairs up, at the other the lecture halls and the entrance to the principal galleries for temporary exhibitions. For them Pei provided a large, essentially shapeless area, articulated for each occasion by an arrangement of temporary partitions. There are limits to the amount of variety such walls can achieve within an extensive space whose floors are uniform, even though the ceiling heights can be varied. These special exhibition galleries can be monotonous. Above all, the place is inescapably and obtrusively a cellar. Not all the advantages of the finest equipment, nor all the skills of the most consistently successful museum display staff in the country can make the space worthy of the greatest loaned objects. Wholly lacking is any suitable preparatory area, inducing in the visitor that moment of quiet anticipatory awe that all great exhibitions deserve.

A national gallery, supported by national tax funds, must serve a national public. In Washington, a large part of the museum-going public are tourists. Pei recognized that the new building would attract large crowds.[19] He believed that many of the visitors to the National Gallery, tourists especially perhaps, were coming for enjoyment. Basic to his scheme was a glazed central court. It should serve as a focus; it should connect one part of the building to another; it should display great works of art; but its essential function would be to establish a mood of

pleasure (fig. 77). From this complex mixture of aluminum and glass hangs the final and largest Calder mobile. And it is emphatically a place of enjoyment. "It is lively and informal. . . . People sit on the planters conversing in normal tones, while kids play on the marble floors." Enjoyable, too, are the varied views from the bridges spanning the space and the pleasures of watching people in motion over them. That these reactions are no accident is revealed by Pei's press conference at the opening of the building. He began by asking the assembled journalists, "Are you enjoying yourselves?"[20] He designed a building where a visitor may, after a time, seek a different experience, perhaps stop at the sales desk, or sit down and talk. He need never become so tired he must rest.

The dominant concept behind the gallery areas was the desire to maintain a domestic scale (fig. 78). Most of them are located one over the other in the three towers that the staff refers to as "houses." Connecting the towers on two sides are several galleries, some often devoted to freestanding sculpture. The contrast between the central space and the galleries is as sharp as the contrast between the great hall of Grand Central Station and the ticket offices and newsstands that surround it. Only three of the gallery areas have natural light (fig. 79), a loss all the more conspicuous because the central space is so amply illuminated.[21]

For some time the catchword in the design of museum galleries has been flexibility. Witness the warehouselike spaces articulated by movable partitions at the Museum of Modern Art or here in the temporary exhibition area of the cellar. The galleries on the upper floors vary in size, shape, and

lighting, and in some cases the ceilings can be adjusted from ten to thirty-five feet.[22] Some are isolated, others linked by exceptionally charming stairways, still others can be connected to make small suites.

To evaluate the interior it may be appropriate to start with a quotation from Colin Amery. "Something strange is happening in the world of art galleries. . . . We have moved into an era where the buildings have become events. In Washington a visitor feels that the great crushes of people in the huge central atrium of the new East Building are there just to wander about in the great space. Their presence has very little to do with the works of art on display, instead it is the I. M. Pei building that . . . they have come to see."[23] The contrast to the Museum of Modern Art, as it was before the latest remodeling, could hardly be sharper.

Those words were written shortly after the building was opened. But long after the novelty has worn off and even after repeated visits, most of the interiors of the East Wing remain exhilarating. Statistics make this point clearly. In 1941–42, its first full year of operation, the National Gallery received just over two million visitors. During the next thirty-five years, although the figures varied surprisingly from year to year, generally they ranged between one and one-half and two million. In the years since the East Wing opened the annual attendance has tripled, leveling off at six to seven million.

If the quality of the spaces cannot be disputed, the balance between them can. The atrium overwhelms the galleries around it. And yet it is so located that psychologically it cannot serve as an introduction to the National Gallery as a whole. The visitor, espe-

cially the repeat visitor, who cares primarily about works of art is likely to ignore the great atrium and at once take the elevator to the top galleries. Yet one always feels that one is retracing one's steps if one proceeds from the East Wing to the West. Perhaps, theoretically, one might have reversed all the relationships, placing the main entrance on Third Street. Practically, in all likelihood this would not have worked.

The most vivid way to appreciate the quality of the interiors of the East Wing is to compare them with those of the original building. There, Colin Amery notwithstanding, a funereal rotunda and a pair of vaulted halls (too slick to be stately) provide the introduction to literally dozens of tight, ill-proportioned galleries, never varying in illumination, varying little in size or shape and rarely in finish.[24] Thank God for the adjacent garden courts. Above all, thank God for the East Wing.

The priorities governing the design of the exterior of the new building were not at all the same as those of the interior. Outside, the essential requirement was that the East Wing should adjust suitably to the original building, and more generally to the traditional image of monumental Washington.[25] Adjust it did, but with at least one curious result. Official regulations required the one entrance to the East Wing to be on Fourth Street. Because of the geo-

76. *National Gallery of Art. East Wing, facade. In the left foreground is a fountain that continues as a waterfall into the restaurant below. Beside the left-hand tower is a sculpture by Henry Moore, commissioned for this space.*

77. *National Gallery of Art. East Wing, central court. Almost everybody seems to be in happy motion; few are standing still admiring the building or the huge late Calder overhead.*

78. *National Gallery of Art. East Wing, painting gallery in one of the towers. Artificially lit, chairless, airless, rarely crowded, these galleries can seem like prison cells for the superb works of art they contain.*

graphical development of Washington most visitors approach the National Gallery from the west. The original building has its entrances on the Mall and on Constitution Avenue. It has become but one in a row of classical revival structures (fig. 73), and unless one deliberately turns to look, one passes by the facade. But, thanks to the plaza, everybody traveling east on Constitution Avenue faces the Fourth Street entrance to the East Wing. As a result, the new building dominates the pair; psychologically, the original has become the extension.[26]

The nature of the site makes it virtually impossible to turn the amorphous hundred-yard-long area between the two buildings into a

place (figs. 73, 76). One long side is defined by the trees of the Mall. Opposite but not parallel to the line of the trees is a row of miscellaneous, not very impressive buildings along Pennsylvania Avenue. Two very busy lanes of traffic intervene. One is therefore only conscious of a sort of broad corridor between the two halves of the gallery. Moreover what is obviously the side door of the West Wing is opposite what is obviously the main door of the East Wing. The surface of the plaza is neither flat nor ordered; instead it is rather a hodgepodge of irregular pyramidal skylights, sprays of water, and a variety of tubes. The pleasant confusion of the area in front does serve to emphasize the severe

79. *National Gallery of Art. East Wing, exhibition of sculpture by David Smith, upper-level gallery of the north tower. The stairs provide isolating pedestals for the individual statues, while their angular and three-dimensional forms emphasize the flat, generally curving planes of the sculpture. The plain walls and uniform ceiling throw the intricacy of the lower half of the photograph into relief. The museum's installation department may be the most admired in the country.*

sculptural simplicity, the pronounced orderliness, of the facade of the East Wing.

Perhaps the greatest interest of this front is its overall arrangement. Not since the Middle Ages has there been such an emphatic twin-towered composition. In detail it is a study of few and simple masses against few and simple voids. It recalls Dudok's work of the early twenties, but formalized, and the elements as brutally reduced in number as they are inflated in scale. Werner Oechslin observed, in a perceptive article, that there is nothing specifically museumlike about the East Wing. The forms would be equally well adapted to the headquarters of a great bank or a Hall of International Congresses.[27]

Intellectually, as a compromise between two styles—modern architecture and the local classical tradition—its closest parallel, perhaps, is Christopher Wren's Tom Tower at Christchurch, Oxford. One of the most popular of Wren's works, this baroque gatehouse is yet Gothic enough in detail to form a suitable entry to Cardinal Wolsey's great cloister court. Like Tom Tower, Pei's East Wing may be admired as an achievement in stylistic virtuosity; but each is the result of an exceptional opportunity, and each is too personal a solution to have exerted or to be likely to exert much influence on later architecture.

Beaubourg

Advanced architecturally, the East Wing of the National Gallery was conventional in its program. This was to expand a major urban art museum, one dedicated to the display of works of art covering a considerable range of time. Inevitably it has been compared to an almost exactly contemporary enterprise in Paris, the Centre National d'Art et de Culture Georges Pompidou. That has been responsibly described as "the only public monument of international quality the 70's have produced."[28] Whether this is true or not, the Center is a type of building Americans do not like, and there has been hardly any comprehensive discussion of it in American publications.[29] Moreover, unlike any recent American museum, the creation of this building was intensely felt as a political issue and the art museum it contained was the most controversial aspect of the broadest and most original cultural enterprise of our times. All these facts justify an exceptionally extended treatment here.

This lengthily titled institution was built in the very middle of Paris on the plateau Beaubourg, and it is now usually called "Beaubourg." The institution was to be radical in its architecture, but this grew out of its program. To understand that requires a brief review of some recent French history.

If Charles de Gaulle's first achievement during his presidency was the solution of the Algerian problem, his second was to initiate a comprehensive revival of France. For a subsequent generation this period is symbolized by the Concorde (an airplane) and La Défense (the new business district just west of the boundary of Paris proper). More generally the sixties represented "the supreme moment of

technological euphoria in Western society: the moment when we genuinely believed that 'freedom' was to be got by providing ourselves with endless power-supplied facility."[30]

Prominent in the French revival were various intellectual initiatives. For some time there had been widespread agreement that "the inadequacy of the cultural infrastructure in our country is manifest, whether in Paris or the provinces." In response to this reaction, André Malraux was appointed the first French minister for cultural affairs. "Malraux is remembered for the cleansing of public buildings in Paris, the development of regional 'Maisons de la Culture,' the decentralisation of the theatre, the creation of Biennales and the creation of the Centre Nationale d'Art Contemporain (CNAC), an agency for stimulating, subsidising and promulgating living art." He also wished to create a new Museum of Modern Art at La Défense and asked Le Corbusier to design it. Le Corbusier objected because he believed "there should be a big cultural centre right in the heart of a working-class area of Paris, where people who do not usually go to museums, theatres or libraries would feel free to walk in."[31] He died before the issue was settled.

Then came the riots of May 1968. In April 1969 de Gaulle resigned, and in June Georges Pompidou was elected to succeed him as president. Of particular consequence were his concern for the rejuvenation of the heart of Paris, his personal interest in the fine arts, and his unusual admiration for monuments. "He once remarked what a shame it was that a man as great as de Gaulle had not left a monument."[32] Pompidou was determined to avoid that mistake.

Late in 1969 he announced his intention to create a new cultural organization in the center of the city. "The President wishes this to be the greatest accomplishment of his term of office, in architecture and content the greatest achievement of our epoch," as a member of his government declared subsequently.[33] The cultural center was to incorporate the first American-style public library in France, a proposal going back to the early sixties, as well as Malraux and Le Corbusier's Museum of Modern Art. Also to be included was a department devoted to the relation of man, industry, and the environment, which grew out of some activities previously carried on at the Museum of Decorative Arts. In 1971 a department dedicated to research into the relationships of acoustics and music was included. There were also to be several suites of galleries for temporary exhibitions, as well as multipurpose auditoria for theater, lectures, concerts, or symposia, spaces for cinematography, a bookstore, and a restaurant. Special attention in some of these departments was to be given to children—a studio for children, a library for children, and so forth.

To sum up the proposal in Pompidou's own words: "It is my dearest wish that Paris have a cultural centre, such as they have tried to create in the United States with so far only partial success. This would be at one and the same time a museum and a centre for artistic creation where, side by side, one would find the plastic arts, music, cinema, books and audio-visual media. This museum could be a museum of modern art only, since the Louvre provides for the art of previous centuries. The art created here would, of course, be modern, and would evolve continually. Thousands of people would use the library and at the same time would come into contact with the arts." As for the location, "Beaubourg

was chosen simply because it was the only site immediately available and I wanted to move fast, convinced that if I waited, nothing would ever happen."[34]

Several broad purposes underlay this proposal, some intellectual, some economic, some social: a regret that in the twentieth century the different areas of knowledge had become increasingly specialized and isolated, coupled with a desire to initiate some reintegration starting with the arts; "a wish to re-establish France as the leading center in the world of creativity in the arts," a position it was widely believed had been lost to New York and London; a desire to revivify the center of the city since so much recent architectural activity had taken place along its inner and outer edges; a concern that the arts should be brought to as wide an audience as possible, especially to the inhabitants of the immediate neighborhood on the one hand, and through exchange of traveling exhibitions to provincial France on the other.[35]

It was a weakness to have so many objectives, but three important factors made it possible to carry out the proposal. First, the determination of Pompidou himself and support from other leading figures, notably Jacques Chirac, François Mitterand, and Robert Bordaz. (The last was a pillar of the French establishment, whose job, as president of the Center, was to get the building built.)[36] Second, the recognition that success in all areas would depend on thorough study by experts, accompanied by an imaginative choice of those men. And finally the awareness that the novelty of the proposal as a whole would demand experiments at every level, from the establishment of Beaubourg as a quasi-independent agency, bypassing traditional bureaucracies, to the use of steel trusses from Krupp

and escalators from Japan, to the employment of a Swede, an Italian, a Yugoslav, and an American among the heads of important departments.[37]

A first decision concerned the site. Since the Middle Ages the main markets of Paris (Halles Centrales) had occupied a large area in the center of the city. The plateau Beaubourg, two blocks totaling some twelve and a half acres, lay directly to its east (fig. 80). An ancient slum, "infectious island no. 1," it had been cleared in the 1930s and thereafter provided parking for the central markets.[38] Since the middle of the nineteenth century a group of metal pavilions had housed the markets. In March 1969 the markets were moved out to Rungis, a southern suburb, and most of the pavilions were torn down, leaving much of the former Halles site vacant.

In this area, including the surviving pavilions, an active popular life developed—speeches, plays, concerts, magicians, a great variety of performances. Meanwhile the City Council and various bureaus of the national government discussed what should be done with the two sites.[39] One important consideration was that the whole densely populated surrounding district had had no park of any kind, nor even a significant open space. Pompidou's declaration of December 11, 1969, resolved several problems: the new cultural center should be placed at Beaubourg and the former market area developed into a trade center. Beneath the latter was to be the major focus of public transportation in Paris, including an improved Métro whose station was ultimately expected to serve thirty thousand people an hour.

A second concern was to define precisely the needs of the various component departments of the center. This involved the forma-

tion of a team composed of architects and engineers, museum curators and librarians, administrators and scientists. By August 1971, after more than two years of intensive work, they had developed a distinctive program.[40]

Meanwhile, an international competition to select an architect was organized in 1970 and announced early in 1971.[41] Of the nine members of the jury only four were French. Despite the fact that the work of the programmers was already far advanced, the competing architects were not constrained by much information. The space required for each of the departments was specified, as was the space needed for services in common. These came to a total of 100,000 square meters. The entire area of ground available was 20,000 square meters. Up to ten thousand people a day were expected to visit the Center, "primarily, the people who live in the district, for whom the presence of the Centre should be a familiar element of their daily lives."[42] The Center should be functional, flexible, "polyvalent," a place where artists and public meet, but where members of the public can themselves become creative.[43]

Early in July 1971 the jury had received some 681 acceptable designs, nearly five hundred of them from forty-nine foreign countries. On the fifteenth they announced the winner, an appropriately international group, the architects Renzo Piano (Italian) and Richard Rogers (English), allied to Ove Arup and Partners, a firm of engineers, Danish in origin.[44] All were

practicing in London. The jury praised the design as straightforward, simple, and full of light (fig. 81). Also, because much of the building was underground, much of the plateau remained available to other forms of recreation.

The competition program had called for "a cultural center for Paris." In order to call attention to a change in emphasis the architects called the design they submitted "a live center of information and entertainment." The proposed building was to be a simple rectangle, more than five hundred feet long and two hundred feet high, located in the northeast edge of the site along the rue du Renard. The available area was to be extended toward the west by abolishing the rue St. Martin.[45] Between the houses on the west side of that street and the rue du Renard there was to be a plaza sloping downward so that it ended some eleven feet below the existing rue du Renard, joining at this point a new underground pedestrian way.

Although it may not have been evident in the drawings submitted for the competition, fundamental to Piano and Rogers' image of Beaubourg was a post-modern concept of urban design. The International Style's urban approach was essentially sculptural. Buildings were conceived as isolated units, for example the Bauhaus, cities as successions of such units, for example Le Corbusier's vision of the remodeling of Paris or Mies' of the business center of Berlin. The greatest masterpieces would survive as museum pieces; otherwise the buildings of the past had no visual contribution to make in urban design.

Rogers, citing with enthusiasm the Piazza della Signoria in Florence and Brunelleschi's approach to preceding architecture, believed instead that the modern should coexist with the past to form a more

varied and active whole. Beaubourg as a sculptural object should address another sculptural object, the only significant building in the area surviving from the past. "To avoid obstructing the view of the sixteenth century Eglise St. Merri to the south, the Boulez Acoustic Research Center is sunk completely underground."[46]

The building proper consisted of a row of paired columns along the rue du Renard and a similar row parallel to it to the west (fig. 82). The outer columns on each side were joined by diagonal wind braces, and the two rows were connected by a series of trusses running without interruption right across the building. The columns supported a glass box that neither touched the ground nor rose to the full height of the columns. This glass box contained six floors of work space and ended in an open roof deck for outdoor exhibitions. Suspended from the columns over part of this deck was a restaurant, and above that mechanical equipment.

Attached to the central columns on the west side was a cluster of glass-enclosed elevators giving access to the various floors; there were also escalators zigzagging from the tower of elevators to some of the floors (figs. 81, 83). These escalators were hung from the columns. Because elevators and escalators were glass-enclosed, the people rising on the face of the building formed a kind of continuum with the people crossing the plaza. The elevators also ran into the ground, connecting the work space with the three floors of parking below (fig. 82). All service functions—elevators for freight and staff, air ducts, electricity ducts, water pipes—were concentrated between the pairs of columns along the rue du Renard.[47] This disposition of corridors and service functions in the ten-foot

80. *Paris. Aerial view of the center of the city, c. 1976. Notre Dame is at upper right; Beaubourg is the bright rectangle at upper left.*

space between the pairs of columns on both facades meant that each floor within was to be a vast rectangular space, 566 feet long unobstructed by vertical elements of any kind. Also in any bay, between adjacent pairs of columns, the height of the floors or ceiling could be changed. Since the usual distance between floor and ceiling was twenty-three feet there was room, throughout the building, to hang mezzanines from the main truss as needed.[48] These were to be secondary spaces to accommodate activities such as storage of works of art or surveillance of visitors. Through all these devices the architects attained one of their principal goals, utmost flexibility.[49]

The building touched the ground only at the columns, a small adjacent entrance lobby, and the service ducts. Otherwise it was raised sufficiently above ground that pedestrians on the rue du Renard could see under it to the full height of the houses on the western edge of the plaza (fig. 84). Thus, in one visual fashion, the building did not interrupt the continuity of the neighborhood. Beneath ground, the building was continued under part of the main plaza and all of a secondary plaza to the south. This space was to be used chiefly for parking, for storage, and for Boulez's Institute of Acoustics and Music.

Such a narrowly architectural description does not suggest what the architects conceived the fundamental purpose of the institution to be: "A Live Center of Information covering Paris and beyond . . . linked up with information dispersal and collection centers throughout France and beyond." In addition to the displays, exhibitions, and performances within, information was to be presented along the major facade, where screens would hang from the columns for "constantly changing information, news, what's in Paris, television, electronic two-way games, etc." (fig. 83).[50] The plaza and the area under the building were to be a horizontal continuation of the facade with "mobile exhibitions, live theater and music, games, meetings, parades, competitions." Around the edge of the plaza there were to be shops, cafes, children's reception areas, design centers, and so forth, while if possible the houses would be converted into "studios and dwellings related to the Center." To sum up: "This Center of constantly changing information is a cross between an information-oriented Times Square

83

82

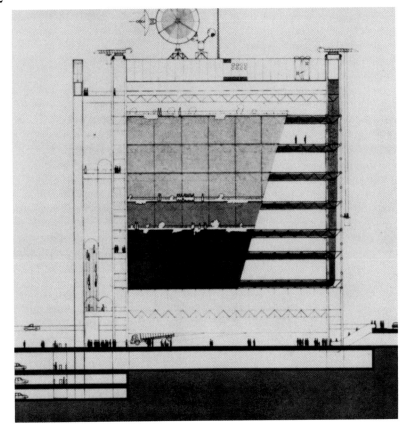

81. Centre National d'Art et de Culture Georges Pompidou ("Beaubourg"), Paris, completed 1977; architects Renzo Piano and Richard Rogers. Model of the design that won the international competition. The building was to be raised on pilotis, the lobby with its elevators forming a free-standing tower connected to the various floors by escalator.

82. Beaubourg. Cross section of the original design. On the right is the rue du Renard, one story above the building's ground floor.

83. Beaubourg. Facade of the original design. Important to the conception of a "Live Center of Information" were images projected on the facade and broadcasts from the roof.

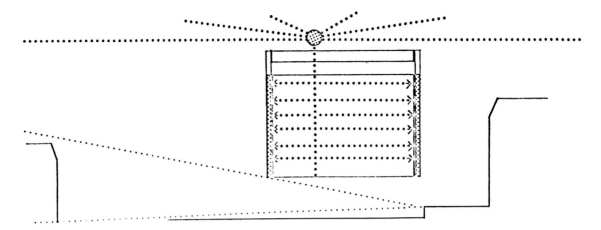

and the British Museum, with stress on two-way participation between people and activities/exhibits."

Pompidou was surprised at the jury's choice, which "he believed was unconsciously influenced by the agitation then taking place over the destruction of the last of the market pavilions." This he himself had recently decreed. He met his architects and "exhorted them to build 'a true architectural monument, one that will be beautiful to the eye.'"[51]

An even greater surprise must have occurred next month when the architects met the team of program planners and read the definitive analysis of the center's requirements these civil servants had at last completed. Together the two groups faced a multitude of difficulties, many of them unanticipated. The French and the English had completely different expectations of the architect's role in completing a building. There were numerous lawsuits instituted by a group of local architects to stop the project entirely.[52] Parisian building regulations demanded substantial changes in the design, and always there was constant pressure to hurry, hurry, hurry.[53] Every group involved with Beaubourg has spoken or written about its experiences with exceptional frankness. The wonder is that the

two multinational groups who shared the primary responsibilities worked together with so little recorded friction.

As a result, the need to make important changes led to a second design, and finally to a return to a modified version of the original proposal. One of Piano and Rogers' crucial innovations was the two great information screens. They were eliminated without explanation. Doubtless expense of operation had something to do with this, but there was a more serious issue. "Who was to vet the texts, choose the pictures?" As with television in France, the government might have chosen to play a major role, but any suggestion of propaganda was an offense to the very idea of a cultural center. "For safety's sake the government insisted on the elimination of the illuminated screens . . . the aim was to prevent the unscheduled appearance of free information."[54]

The adjustable ceilings were abandoned; there was not time enough to work out the engineering details. The most regrettable alterations resulted from French laws of fire prevention and control. These forced the abandonment of the pilotis, so that the building now rests on the ground (fig. 85). Moreover the total height had to be reduced from almost two hun-

dred feet to one hundred forty; there was one less upper floor.[55]

Aesthetically the effects were disastrous. Somewhat more activity had to be concentrated within a smaller glass container. What suffered were the proportions. The largest spaces in the building are 166 feet wide and 344 feet long; such spaces need to be more than twenty-three feet high, especially if ten of those feet are taken up by lattice beams between which wind a multitude of ducts, varying in function, size, and color (fig. 86). The more subdivided the space (as in offices and the galleries of the permanent collections) the more depressing the effect. Fortunately, the forum has a double height as do a few other areas in the building. These are among the few exhilarating monumental interiors created since World War II (figs. 87, 93).

As executed, both rows of supporting members are outside the glazed envelope and the pairs of equal columns have been replaced by unequal pairs, each consisting of a column and a vertical bar (figs. 85, 88, 91). A vertical series of short horizontal beams project from each column, constituting rocker arms, known locally as "gerberettes."[56] The outer section of the gerberette is some four times as long as the inner, and the junction with the column is a semicircular

84. *Beaubourg. Architects' sketch showing how the building as originally designed would not block the view from the plaza.*

85. *Beaubourg. The building as executed, from the northwest. A single run of escalators hangs like the gangway of a ship across the entire west facade.*

86. *Beaubourg. The library.*

opening around a pin. The short end of the gerberette is fastened into the end of the main truss. Thus, transmitted through the gerberettes, the row of columns carries the entire weight of the building.[57] The weight would tend to rotate the gerberettes, raising their outer arms. This tendency is counteracted by the vertical bars attached to the outer arms of the gerberettes and anchored into the ground (fig. 88). Since steel is stronger in tension than in compression the vertical bars need only be eight inches in diameter, whereas the columns are thirty-four. Additional horizontal and diagonal bars are attached to the ends of the gerberettes stabilizing the whole structure against wind and other pressures (fig. 85). As a final precautionary measure against fires, the columns are filled with a circulating system of water; also if a fire occurs water is automatically sprayed from the top down the glass walls of the building.

Because the building rests upon the ground the whole reception hall has been moved inside. A single pair of up and down escalators, enclosed in a glass tube, is hung from the outside network of bars (fig. 85). Starting at ground level at the north and rising to the top floor at the south, it has been aptly compared to a gangway hung against the hull of a ship. Horizontal gangway tubes hanging under the gerberettes give access to various entrances on each floor (fig. 91).

Seen from the west, the effect is of a simple huge glass prism enveloped in a shiny spider's web of steel bars (fig. 85).[58] Exotic in shape, elegant in form, and having the functional inevitability of a traditional hand tool, the gerberettes are especially striking (fig.

87. *Beaubourg. A gallery for temporary exhibitions, two stories high.*

88. *Beaubourg. The south end of the building.*

88).[59] Closing the small subsidiary plaza to the south is the late Gothic parish church of St. Merri (figs. 91, 92). The twisting flamboyant tracery of its windows, the sharp projection of its gargoyles sustain a refreshing dialogue with the multiplicity of bars and the orderly succession of gerberettes at the cultural center.

The facade along the rue du Renard is even more striking (fig. 89).[60] A gaudy succession of ninety-odd vertical ducts—red for elevators (people), blue for air conditioning, green for water, yellow for electricity—are held in a

single neat bundle by the silver rods sustaining the building. The colors are primary; the succession apparently haphazard, but, this being France, doubtless ordained by some hidden logic. Elderly, standard Parisian buildings line the rue du Renard. Their lack of distinction is relieved only by the more-than-ordinary busyness of the inhabitants and a distant lateral glimpse of the solemn towers of Notre Dame. Beaubourg is a boisterous interruption. Viewed from this side it seems less like a building than an enormous intricate machine. It is also a startling reminder that impressive artifacts exist that pique our curiosity precisely because they are so apart from the pressure of our cares.

On January 15, 1975, the French Assembly voted to establish Pompidou's Center. The left abstained *en bloc.* What else could they have done? For years they had criticized right-wing governments for not allocating sufficient funds to cultural activities, and yet they could not trust the use this government would make of the new funds. An initial objection was that the minister concerned had not supplied them with sufficient information; later they came to the conclusion that this was because the project had not been properly thought through. For the moment a prominent Communist deputy felt confined to voicing a general distrust in "a cultural policy whose watchwords remain authoritarianism, arbitrariness and skimping."[61]

As the institution's intentions became clearer, criticisms became both more intense and more precise. Pompidou expressed the hope that between Beaubourg and the central markets a quarter dominated by the arts and culture would develop by contagion. But exactly the same vision could be perceived in a different light. The left foresaw the quarter trans-

formed by the manipulations of the local Chamber of Commerce; the working class driven out by renovations, to be replaced by those better off, after developers had pocketed substantial capital gains; the commercial landscape radically changed; boutiques, restaurants, and art galleries moving in, speculating on the new cultural vocation of the quarter, attracted by the vision of all sorts of clients drawn in by the future Center. "Paris-New York" was the name chosen for the opening exhibition in 1977. This, it was said, would increase European demand for American-owned art and enable collectors across the Atlantic to unload their stock at top prices.[62]

Basically, Malraux's policy had been to foster culture in the French provinces. Beaubourg represents a reaction in favor of Paris.[63] The cost of constructing the building was $100,000,000. The proposed operating budget was $34,000,000. This was slightly more than the cost of all the other French national museums put together. Some $2,000,000 a year was allocated for the purchase of works of art, half the total spent for this purpose by the state.[64] All told, the French national museums

89. *Beaubourg. The east facade on the rue du Renard, a startling interruption to the dreariness of a middle-sized Parisian business street.*

90. *Beaubourg. Plans of various floors as executed. The forum occupies the central space on the ground floor and basement (5). The basement space below the plaza is for vehicle access and parking (1, 2). The rows of columns and rods supporting the building are visible in the ground-floor and basement plans. Interior escalators unite sections of departments; the main escalator, outside, begins on the ground floor at top right and rises toward the left.*

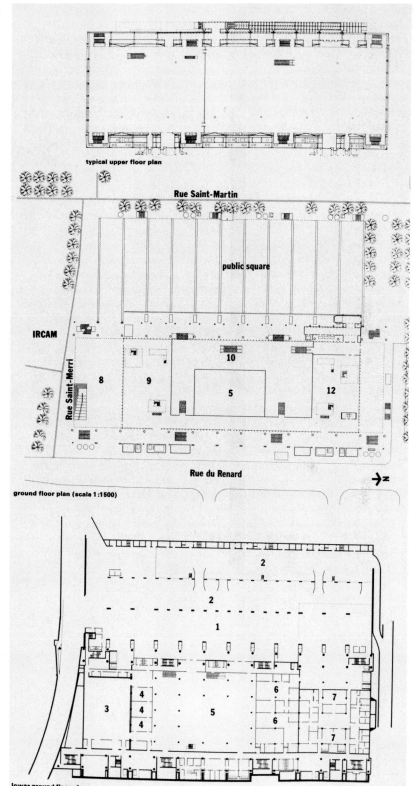

employed 1,500 people. Of these, 1,200 were already working in the Parisian region. The addition of a thousand employees at Beaubourg would throw the situation even further out of balance. Finally, by making the staff of Beaubourg independent of the bureaucratic apparatus of the ministries of Culture and Education and answerable only to the ministers themselves, this group of employees was shut off from all those devices that had slowly evolved to guarantee individual civil servants their professional independence when confronting their political masters.[65]

Even the fundamental intellectual concepts behind Beaubourg were called into question. The interrelationship of the arts was mocked. "As if the indiscriminate juxtaposition of aesthetic activities was going to produce (by chemical precipitation?) new insights, new themes, new genres. As if you couldn't read Joyce unless you were sitting on a Ruhlmann chair, in a room full of Braques, to the strains of Webern." Beaubourg was compared to a supermarket, designed for the masses to consume culture rather than reflect upon it.[66] Finally it was also rejected as elitist.

Needless to say the building did not escape criticism even before it was open. The line supposedly taken by the architects was "to parody technological efficiency, to mimic, in the midst of gratuitousness and make-believe, the smooth-running wheels of industry. . . . A box, a plain box, to house a programme that is equally clear, all light and no shadow. . . . The building—even though its effects of mass classify it as a piece of brand-image architecture, of architecture as advertisement—is presented as the ultimate in functionalism, when it would be truer to call it a functionalist *reductio ad absurdum*. Of the aesthetic developed at Gropius's Bauhaus at Dessau in the 1920s . . . all that remains here is the bombast of a construction based on one idea alone, that of sheer size. Load-bearing girders 50 metres long, giving clear open spaces 7,500 square metres in area—this is the achievement we are invited to applaud."[67]

Le Monde put it succinctly: "Beaubourg is an anthology of ugliness."[68]

Beaubourg opened on February 2, 1977. How, in fact, does it work? Beneath the plaza and the building itself extends a bus terminal, parking for seven hundred cars, storage not only for supplies but for thousands of works of art, workshops, and all the facilities needed to serve a library dedicated to providing an endless succession of the latest books, tapes, and photographs, as well as meeting the demands of preparing several unending series of temporary exhibitions. Under the small square to the south are all the offices, workshops, laboratories, and concert halls for Boulez's Institute of Acoustics and Music (fig. 92).[69]

Entering the building from the plaza you look down into a forum, a vast place of welcome, forty-seven feet high and covering more than 12,000 square feet (fig. 93). The floor below you is underground, but at the level where the people coming by bus, taxi, or car enter the Center (fig. 91). The forum provides welcome, but hardly orientation; indeed at times it is intoxicatingly confusing. For example, at one visit the whole center of it was given over to a vast articulated sculpture of a giant by Tinguely, Niki de Saint-Phalle, and Bernard Luginbuhl, a "kokodrome," no less, they declared.[70] In and out ran an electric train, child-size and children-crammed. The giant contained a "shop for aberrations" representing Daniel Spoerri's thoughts on the fetishes of the art market. The message of the forum seems to be that you don't always have to be so serious about culture, or in the architects' words, "the building itself is a fun-palace."[71]

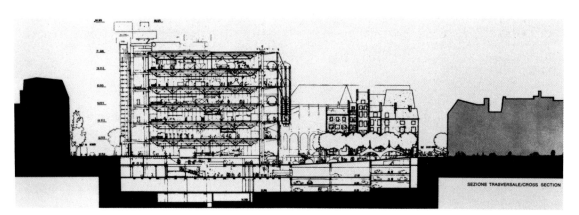

SEZIONE TRASVERSALE/CROSS SECTION

Unforgettable, around the forum, were the subsidiary spaces: an excellent bookstore, a subsidiary library dedicated to the latest books, records, newspapers, and magazines, all presented by their publishers, a gallery for the exhibition of strictly contemporary art, another for the latest in industrial design, a studio for children, devoted to the cultivation of the senses, and not far away a small library for children.[72] Slowly one realized that in these spaces at the fringe of the forum were foreshadowed all the major activities going on elsewhere in the building.

The bulk of the second, third, and fourth floors are given over to the library, while the remainder of the third and fourth and all of the

91. *Beaubourg. Cross section of the building as executed. On the left the service activities appear outside the frame of the building. On the right, round corridors run across the facade at each floor, between the columns and the rods; the escalator runs outside the rods. Further right and behind is the church of St. Merri.*

92. *Beaubourg. Longitudinal section as executed. This illustrates the depth of the Institute of Acoustics and Music, five full floors under the plaza at right.*

fifth are devoted to the Museum of Modern Art (figs. 95, 96). Internal escalators link the various library and museum floors to one another. The top floor contains space for temporary exhibitions, a bar, a restaurant, and terraces for the display of sculpture and the enjoyment of a superlative panorama of Paris. Offices are scattered about, usually near the spaces for which their occupants are responsible. The offices have the same fixed ceiling height as the public spaces (fig. 94), their furniture—every piece down to the last wastepaper basket designed by Piano and Rogers—seeming lost in the vast unarticulated space. "Uncluttered" by partitions, they seem as dreary as those fluorescent-lit supermarket offices in which so many were condemned to work in wartime. But this criticism reflects a change in the program during the course of construction. No such extent of offices was part of the original conception, and, appropriately, offices are now being moved out to a neighboring building.

An institution so dedicated to contemporary life leads an exceptionally changing existence. It is perhaps presumptuous for a foreigner who necessarily visits it only now and then to attempt an assessment. Certainly, at the start, the government assembled an excep-

tional group of department heads, for example Jean-Pierre Seguin for the library; Pontus Hulten, lured from Stockholm, to take over the museum; Pierre Boulez resigning as music director of the New York Philharmonic to found the Institute of Acoustics and Music. Not all of the original luminaries have remained. (One even left but has since returned in a different capacity.) It is certainly too soon to comment comprehensively on the achievement of their successors.

One primary series of facts should be mentioned. The program sent to the competing architects suggested that the Center might have an attendance of up to 10,000 people a day;[73] by its second year it was averaging almost 22,000, with a maximum of 50,000 and an annual total approaching seven million. Access to the upper floors of this most flexible of buildings is not adapted to such unexpected crowds, and on some Sundays one must wait twenty minutes to get a place on the escalator. The library (fig. 86) was provided with 1,300 chairs. It has an average daily attendance approaching 13,000 readers. The art museum must, by law, charge an admission fee, which restricts its average daily attendance to 3,100. But on Sundays admission is free and averages 13,400 visi-

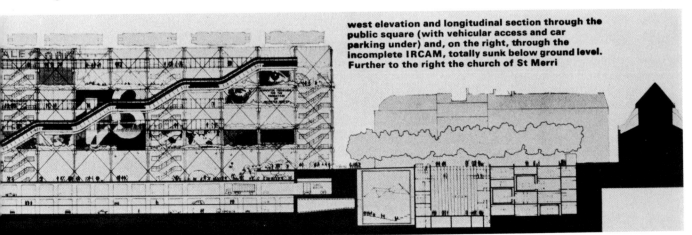

west elevation and longitudinal section through the public square (with vehicular access and car parking under) and, on the right, through the incomplete IRCAM, totally sunk below ground level. Further to the right the church of St Merri

tors, while the annual total, approaching 1,585,000, exceeds that of the Museum of Modern Art in New York.

The nature of Beaubourg's visitors is interesting. Most of the users of the library are high school and college students. They have little interest in other activities going on in the Center. Forty percent of the visitors to the museum are foreigners, and those who attend the museum take a greater interest in other activities of the Center than do any other identifiable group.[74] This is doubly ironic. A basic purpose of the institution was to break down the barriers between intellectual fields, and in all the extensive enthusiastic literature about the Center before it opened, its potential contribution to foreigners is almost never mentioned.

The various activities intended for the young are limited to three hundred children a day, between the ages of four and twelve.[75] They were intended for those from the immediate neighborhood. By the second year of operation the demand was greater than the Center could accommodate.

The Museum of Modern Art in Beaubourg has some 264,000 square feet for the exhibition of art, far more than in New York's Museum of Modern Art even after its recent expansion. Under Pontus Hulten's directorship the museum undertook comprehensive shows of the work of individual artists, notably the inaugural exhibition of Marcel Duchamp. More unusual were three exhibitions devoted to the relationship of Paris to other centers of artistic activity: "Paris-New York"; "Paris-Berlin"; "Paris-Moscow." Each of these exhibitions was accompanied by an impressive catalogue.

Much less satisfactory has been the display of the permanent collection of twentieth-century paintings and sculpture. This is the largest assemblage in Europe, numbering originally some eight thousand objects including two thousand pieces of sculpture. (The collection almost doubled over the next decade). Of these, a varying group of about eleven hundred are on public exhibition. Another of six hundred are available to specialists. They are hung on racks, extending upwards from normal ceiling level. For proper viewing an attendant lowers the racks by pushing a button. The remainder of the collection is in storage, much of it directly below in the reinforced-concrete basement.

The architects had had little experience with exhibiting works of art and, like Mies, Richard Rogers believes that decisions on this subject should be the responsibility of the curator. The original intention was that the paintings should be displayed on relatively small screens hung from the ceiling or perhaps raised from the floor on metal legs. It is not hard to imagine what a confusion many hundreds of pictures displayed in this way would have created. Instead, much of the great expanse of floor space was filled with a series of three-sided temporary huts, painted white and given the scale of small rooms (fig. 95). These were arranged in clusters so that objects could be displayed in appropriate groups. Contact with the individual object could be satisfactory enough, but the total effect was flimsy and denigrating. The disparity between the quality of the objects and that of the backgrounds was so distressing that several collectors refused to allow their actual or promised gifts to be displayed at Beaubourg. Moreover it proved too expensive to change the means of presentation frequently as had been the original plan. The huts and screens that were intended to be temporary became quasi-permanent, dirty and damaged.[76]

Add to all this the inadequate facilities provided from the start for film and video, for conferences and seminars. Clearly there was too great a disparity between the success of the institution and the inadequacy of its facilities. Something had to be done.

Plans for substantial remodeling were announced in January 1984. The administrative offices of the center are gradually being moved into adjacent structures. The space so gained is being devoted to a variety of purposes, notably seminar and conference rooms, in addition to a center of information concerning artistic events in regional France as well as in foreign countries. A new entrance has been provided at the southwest corner of the building. Orientation has been improved.

Under the guidance of Renzo Piano, one of the original architects, the building proper has been enlarged by one bay underground at the north, accommodating a new 345-seat cinema with a screen thirty-one feet long; with its separate entrance it can be kept open twenty-four hours a day. At the south end, the enclosed portion of the building has been extended by two bays on the ground floor, increasing the space devoted to contemporary art from 10,000 square feet to 19,800. One of these bays has been set aside for experimental art, or at least for "the art of today." The entry to the museum proper has been transferred to the fifth floor, whose entire space is devoted to art between 1905 and 1960. The fourth floor is shared with the library, the museum's portion displaying art since 1960.

93. *Beaubourg. The forum. Usually it is thronged with people.*

94. *Beaubourg. A typical office.*

95. *Beaubourg. A gallery in the Museum of Modern Art as originally installed.*

96. *Beaubourg. Gae Aulenti's proposed reinstallation of the fifth floor.*

Dominique Bozo, at that time director of the museum, wished to rearrange the galleries. The Italian interior designer Gae Aulenti was commissioned to undertake this task. Basic demands were that the display should be more homogeneous than previously and that the spaces should be closer to the bourgeois interiors for which most of the works had been designed.[77] She created on the fifth floor a near-central corridor running the length of the building. Sculpture terraces are provided at either end and opposite the middle of one side. Flanking this corridor are rooms varying in size and shape but uniformly fifteen feet high. These are principally devoted to paintings. Under each of the twelve transverse beams is a cross corridor some six feet wide with walls ten feet high and a pedimented glass ceiling rising to a thirteen-and-a-half-foot peak (fig. 96). The walls of these cross corridors might have niches or display cases some two feet deep. In them are placed smaller objects or drawings, prints, and photographs relating to the paintings in nearby rooms. The great trusses with their intersecting ducts, still visible in the rest of the building, are on the fifth floor now largely obscured by a complex variety of false ceilings. Special attention has been given to lighting. Sculpture is spotlit; otherwise light is uniformly diffused along the walls. This makes it possible to change displays without altering the illumination.

A number of consequences of these alterations should be pointed out. The remodeling mollified the collectors who had objected to having their works of art displayed at Beaubourg. The execution of this brilliant compromise has increased the amount of wall space available for display by a third. The striking views of the city from the sculpture gardens serve to re-

late the esoteric world of a modern art museum to ordinary life. Over the long run much will depend on how successfully the light-weight walls and ceilings withstand the wear and tear from millions of visitors and how well their present immaculate surfaces are maintained.

The very possibility of such radical transformation exemplifies the principle of flexibility on which Piano and Rogers' design was based. To paraphrase: Institutions constantly develop and change, while constructions are more enduring. Buildings should not unduly restrain change; flexible buildings should be changed when necessary. The architects welcome Gae Aulenti's transformation of the museum.[78]

Beaubourg is the result of extraordinary collaborations. None of the published literature gives an adequate evaluation of the contribution made by each of the dozens of individuals involved. Striking was Pompidou's premise that the principal artistic achievements of an epoch share basic characteristics and that the presentation of all in one building can enhance the understanding of each. Remarkable was his decision to select a large site in the very heart of what recurrently over some eight centuries has been the most cultivated city in Europe. Impressive, too, was his economic understanding and idealism. "The nation should provide the means, then, and leave action to the genius of its time and people. Waste is worth more in matters like this than the determination to spend money prudently. In sum, you don't put much down, and the stake is immense."[79]

To the design team belongs the credit of adopting the tradition of a metal and glass building. Hitherto associated with recreational or commercial structures like greenhouses, the Crystal Palace, or de-

partment stores, they adapted it to a permanent and major urban working building, and in the process endowed Paris with its most playful monument, containing a few grand and exhilarating interiors. The idea of Beaubourg as a "live vehicle of information"—all its departments using all the interior spaces to act in unison; the moving images on both main facades as well as the activities in both piazze simultaneously conveying related messages—that is an original and grand concept. As the architects have described the situation, "We have always thought of the piazza as a space that mediates between the building and its surroundings . . . a place where things were continually happening. . . . The client was much more keen on having a grand open space to view the building from. The point is that we saw the building as a dynamic thing, whereas the users seem to see it more as a static, monumental thing."[80]

It is true that constraints of politics and budgets eliminated their major innovation, the electric news screen on the facades; but there was no mention of money in the circular issued to the competitors. On the contrary, the venture was advertised to the participants as a contest of ideas. In this context the "live vehicle of information" served its purpose: this was the idea that won.

The Sackler Museum at Harvard

Beaubourg has repeatedly been characterized as the terminal monument in the megastructure architectural movement of the mid-1960s.[81] Harvard's Arthur M. Sackler Museum is a striking example of the convergence of the modern and the traditional in contemporary art, or as its architect James Stirling has written, "it combines the abstract and the representational in art museum architecture."[82] This building rejects not only the concept of open galleries articulated by temporary screens, but also virtually all the well-known attributes of the International Style. Instead it returns to a traditional spatial vocabulary and fenestration; it features familiar materials—brick, bluestone, rough stucco, brass, and oak—rather than those that project an aura of high technology; it is also greatly concerned to relate with immediately surrounding structures that

were built over a span of more than a century and exemplify half a dozen different styles (fig. 98).

Although in functional terms the Sackler is a self-sufficient entity, it owes its existence to Harvard's need to expand its Fogg Art Museum and broadly considered must be viewed in conjunction with that older institution.

The Fogg is Harvard's principal art museum (fig. 98, extreme right). It contains collections of paintings, sculpture, drawings, and prints from many schools of Oriental, ancient, European, and American art. It includes the full range of museum services but also a large art library (photographs, slides, and books) as well as the classrooms and offices of the university's Fine Arts Department.

Basic to the original program for the Fogg was the belief that every aspect of the study of art should be under one roof. Students were to compare originals in the collection to photographs of similar objects elsewhere, listen to formal lectures concerning them, discuss them in a class in the galleries, read about them while facing them, watch them being conserved in a labora-

tory, and paint their own pictures when inspired by them. Except for the last-named function, which was taken over by the Carpenter Center for the Visual Arts next door, all other elements in the program have remained in effect to this day.

The original Fogg Museum was replaced by the present neo-Georgian structure on a different site. This opened in 1927 and has been enlarged twice since: by a small wing containing a lounge, library offices, and the carpenter's shop and by an underground extension of the book stacks. But, after half a century of growth of the collections, the staff, and the student body, every activity in the building had become appallingly cramped for space.

One of Daniel Robbins' first acts upon assuming the directorship of the Fogg in 1971 was to initiate discussion of an extension to the

97. *Cambridge, Massachusetts. Site plan showing the Arthur M. Sackler Museum in relation to other buildings.*

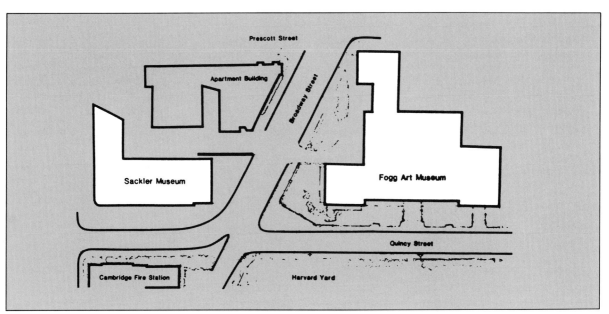

museum. Seymour Slive, who succeeded Robbins in 1974, continued these efforts and obtained funding for new construction as well as for remodeling the existing building. In addition he was obliged to raise an endowment to support the operation of both buildings and to improve the salaries of the staff. Fortunately, a site became available across Broadway, immediately to the north of the Fogg (figs. 97, 98), and Dr. Arthur M. Sackler of New York offered to underwrite the cost of a separate new museum.

The senior staff of the museum, acting as a program committee, recommended relocating the galleries, storerooms, and offices of four curatorial departments (Oriental, Islamic, Ancient, and Textiles) into the new building along with the museum's photographic studios, publication and membership offices, and about half the classrooms and professorial offices of the Fine Arts Department. To be included also were galleries for temporary exhibitions, a library devoted to Oriental art, the registrar's department, and the superintendent's quarters. From the start

it was hoped that there would be a connection between the two buildings, so that these last-named functions might serve both. However, each can operate without this link. These decisions made, the staff prepared a 234-page statement of the museum's needs to serve as a program for the architect.

Architects for Harvard's buildings are appointed by the university's Corporation, in effect the executive committee of its board of trustees, but the separate schools and divisions are given much freedom in the nomination of designers. In recent decades there has been no consistent policy concerning architecture, and the results have been uneven. The Fogg Museum staff was determined that an outstanding architect should be chosen for the new building. To this end, a large committee was formed under the chairmanship of Seymour Slive. This included members of the museum staff, Harvard administrators, and professors (including the author). It reviewed the work of some eighty-four architects, American and foreign, and ultimately recommended the dis-

tinguished British firm of James Stirling, Michael Wilford and Associates, whom the Corporation appointed.

Even in 1979, when he was chosen, James Stirling was notable among present-day architects as an originator. He is also concerned with the adjustment of new buildings to their surviving older neighbors. In addition he had at that time made a number of designs for art museums, including a scheme for an art gallery at the University of St. Andrews in Scotland (fig. 100). Here he planned to add curving wings to a charming eighteenth-century house with a porter's lodge on one side and a later structure on the other. His proposal offered an appealing unification of the old and the new.

Stirling began by making sketches.[83] One complex early sketch showed plans of a gallery floor in black: a sequence of clearly

98. *Sackler Museum, completed 1985; architect James Stirling. The architect's presentation drawing showing the Sackler's relation to the Fogg Art Museum.*

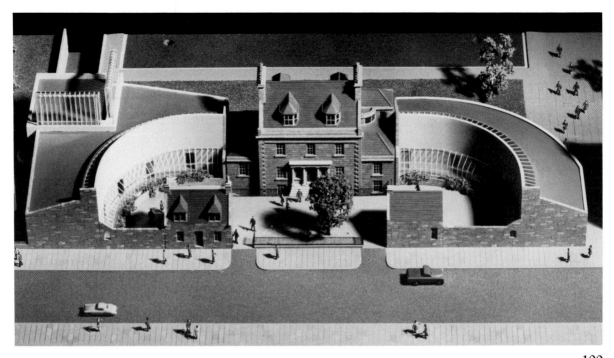

100

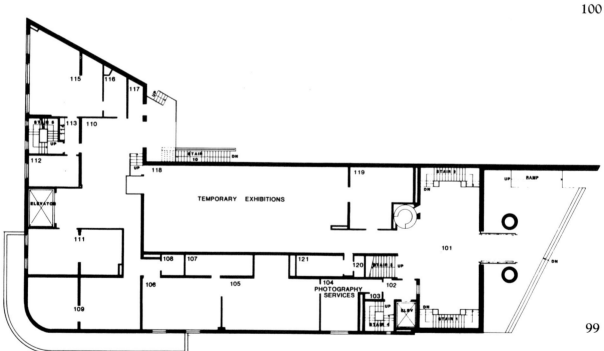

99

99. *Sackler Museum. Ground-floor plan. The entrance is at right, with the machinery room beneath the triangular plaza.*

100. *James Stirling, model for a proposed expansion to create an art building for the University of St. Andrews, Scotland, 1971.*

defined rectangular and circular spaces (fig. 101). The idea of the galleries as a loft broken up by temporary partitions was ruled out from the start. On the same sheet was a series of bird's-eye views of prismatic units in red, revealing that he was thinking of interior and exterior arrangements simultaneously but sometimes independently. One later study showed an attempt to duplicate the basic arrangement of the Fogg, with a glazed central court surrounded by galleries. Eventually this court evolved into the Sackler's skylit grand staircase. As the final scheme gradually took form, Stirling tried out similar features that echoed other nearby buildings. Thus at one point he designed a great semicircular arch, leading from the lobby to the main stairs and the ground-floor galleries. Clearly this was a reflection of the entrance to H. H. Richardson's nearby Sever Hall, a building Stirling particularly admires. A final step was to sketch a series of alternate facades approximating such traditional styles as Egyptian, Greek, or Oriental. His thought was to suggest the nature of one of the collections within. All that survives of this approach are the two cylindrical towers in front of the main facade that seem to symbolize the idea of entrance (figs. 98, 104).

As a complement to these aesthetic experiments, Stirling, right from the start, showed himself concerned to meet the specifications set out in the detailed program the Fogg Museum had prepared. Committee meetings with him discussed at length variations of a foot here and a foot there between the requirements of the program and the design he was at any given moment proposing. The building of the Sackler Museum had its problems, but these never involved relations between the ar-

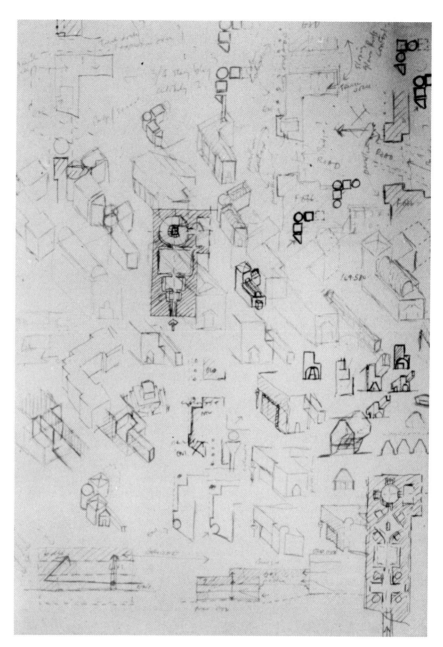

101. *Sackler Museum. Part of a sheet of early sketches by James Stirling. The lighter figures (drawn in red) are bird's-eye studies of the exterior conceived as a group of geometric volumes. The darker figures (drawn in black) are later and include two hatched ground plans. These completely disregard the underlying red drawings. However, in both sets of sketches Stirling was thinking of the building not in modern terms as a simple warehouselike entity, but in post-modern terms with each major space constituting a self-contained independent unit.*

chitect and his ultimate client, the professional staff of the Fogg.

At Harvard, the environment of the L-shaped site influenced the design of the Sackler Museum in several ways (figs. 97, 98, 104). Stirling wished the new building to approximate the height of the adjacent Fogg and of neighboring buildings. This determined its sixty-foot elevation. Because students and visitors would normally approach the Museum along Quincy Street, the main entrance was placed near the southwest corner of the property, facing the north end of the Fogg. Local building codes restrict the size of the building to sixty thousand square feet of floor space; they also require truck maneuvering to take place on the site, so the service driveway runs diagonally across the lot from Cambridge Street to Broadway. Quincy Street slopes in such a way that the north end of the Fogg is raised substantially above the street (fig. 98). As the Sackler's floor is slightly below ground level, a proposed bridge beginning at the Fogg's second-floor level will someday link its principal suite of galleries to those of the top floor of the new museum (fig. 105). Zoning regulations also stipulate that a considerable portion of the site for the new building be left open. Near the southeast boundary of the lot is an apartment house between the Fogg and the Sackler. Here the Sackler building is set back from the property line so as not to deprive the apartments of too much light (figs. 97, 98).

The program called for many rooms of two different heights: galleries and some storerooms fourteen or more feet and offices about eight and a half feet. Stirling designed an L-shaped building with a central circulation spine dividing three floors of galleries and storerooms on the inner side of the L from five floors of library, offices,

storage, and classrooms along the outer (figs. 102, 103). A dramatic stairway leads straight upwards from the entrance lobby to the top-floor galleries. Landings give access on one side to the second-floor gallery, and on the other to several levels of offices connected by corridors (figs. 102, 106). An elevator and service stairs at the ends of the corridors provide additional access to the office floors.

Although constructed of concrete block, the new museum, like the Fogg and, indeed, the majority of buildings at Harvard, is sheathed in brick (figs. 98, 104). The brick on the southwest wall forming the entrance facade is uniformly a buff color, but a large panel of stucco, divided into rectangles suggesting outsize rustications, surrounds the entrance. Standing free are two tall concrete cylinders that mark the doorway in a monumental manner, at the same time serving the building's central air conditioning system and ventilating its equipment room beneath the triangular plaza (fig. 99). The vestibule between the cylinders is built of glass panels. Its truncated A-frame roof is reflected in the shape of the entrance doorway. Above is a large square window, which is to become the entrance to the bridge that will someday connect the new structure to the Fogg. Until then the window brightens the important gallery of Chinese bronzes and jades. The brick of the entrance facade continues a short distance around the corner on the Quincy Street side, so that the whole front is a distinctive pavilion preceding the bulk of the building. Owing to the shape of the site, the location of adjoining buildings, and the screen of buildings along the driveway, the elevations on the inner sides of the L are little noticed.

The character of the exterior along Quincy and Cambridge

Streets is governed by the fenestration. The rooms behind the outer sides of the L are a mixture of offices, seminar rooms, and study-storage areas varying in size. Characteristically, Stirling centered windows in most of these rooms to make the interiors more inviting. The rooms adjoin one another in functional sequences, with the result that on the exterior the windows are irregularly spaced, and the spacings differ markedly from floor to floor (figs. 98, 99, 104, 106). Treated conventionally, the facades on Quincy and Cambridge Streets would be uniform brick surfaces upon which are scattered a haphazard array of shiny glass rectangles, varying in width. Instead, Stirling divided the outer wall into contrasting bands, the windows being set against graphite-gray bricks, the intervening bands being the same orange buff as the facade pavilion. The outer angle of the L, where Cambridge and Quincy Streets meet, has been markedly curved. As a result the west and north facades create the impression of a single continuous surface bending around a corner.

The facades of the inner side of the L are virtually windowless, offering Stirling the opportunity to create an almost unbroken wall,

102. *Sackler Museum. Axonometric drawing.*

103. *Sackler Museum. Cross section. The lecture hall was added after the main outlines of the* parti *had been determined. It had to be wider than the galleries; this required cantilevering the support of the right-hand wall of the main stairway. Columns in the lecture hall reduce the length of the cantilever; a barrel vault hides the cantilever beams. On the second gallery floor, a single bay window brings natural light to the central gallery.*

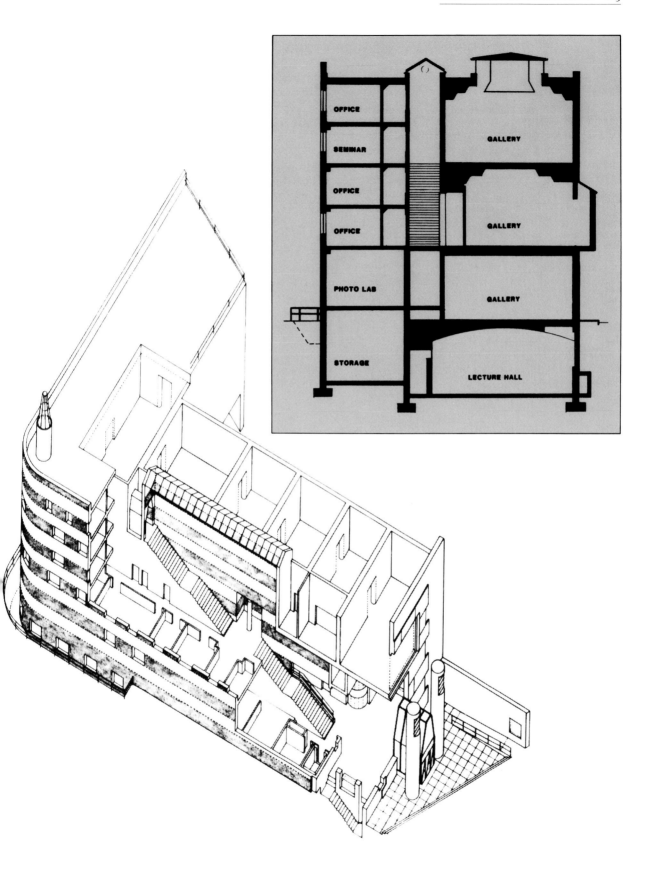

OFFICE

SEMINAR

OFFICE

OFFICE

PHOTO LAB

STORAGE

GALLERY

GALLERY

GALLERY

LECTURE HALL

104. *Sackler Museum from Quincy Street.*

some sixty feet high, whose character would be defined entirely by the quality of the brick chosen and the skill with which it was laid. The unphotographable result is magnificently sensuous in itself and a splendid light reflector into the rooms of the adjacent apartment house.

There remained the facade facing up Quincy Street (fig. 104). This posed a double, and perhaps an insoluble problem. On the one hand the design must be satisfactory whether the building was free-standing or whether it was the recipient of a one-story bridge across Broadway. The bridge in itself was to be a considerable structure, longer, in fact, than the facade of the Sackler along Quincy Street.

The second consideration was more subtle. Psychologically, if not statistically, the Sackler was divided in two, half being five stories of offices, classrooms, and storage,

the other half being three stories of exhibition galleries. Two stories of the latter were artificially lit, the remainder skylit. Only on the Quincy Street facade could the scale of the gallery half of the building be expressed. The result is that the facade is treated as an independent pavilion that reflects the scale of the gallery segment of the building and deliberately contrasts with the scale of the curatorial and academic segment of the building (figs. 98, 104). Final judgment of the design must be deferred until the present building comes visually into its own, until the Sackler becomes physically, as it is already intellectually, a part of the Fogg.

The entrance to the Sackler Museum leads through the glass vestibule facing Broadway. From this the visitor passes into a severe, monumental hall (figs. 99, 102, 107). It is surprisingly tall: thirty-four feet. The walls of rough

stucco continue the huge rustication of the entrance front. Turning left or right, to follow the main axis of the room, one sees a pair of slender piers, startlingly white against the off-white walls, and behind them, at ceiling level, a long strip window providing the room with ample light. Below the window is a brise-soleil. The severity of the space is unexpected after the mellow warmth of the exterior; the viewing point is unusual. We ordinarily expect our first experience of a long rectangular space to be from a narrow end, the way we first see the nave of a church, for example. In fact, entering a long room at a central cross axis has historical precedents; it was a favorite nineteenth-century device, derived from the classical tradition.

Right and left, behind the piers, are stairways leading down to an impressive lecture hall seating 285 (figs. 99, 103, 107). Mornings, in term time, for some ten minutes every hour when classes are changing, a horde of students will descend one of these stairways while a comparable group will mount up the other. Since most of the lectures are illustrated with slides, the lecture hall too is a long rectangle in plan, though in this case entered from a corner. The seats drop away in a familiar gentle slope; the pink ceiling is the shallowest of barrel vaults with an aisle on the left defined by a row of five columns, sturdy, chamfered cylinders, devoid of decoration. These columns do, in fact, support the east half of the building, and they look it. On the opposite side, on the right, the wall and adjacent ceiling are cut away to form what Stirling calls "a psychological window," a shallow niche that suggests fenestration in the otherwise windowless and subterranean space. It can serve also for the occasional display of a large, horizontal work of art—painting, tapestry, or ceramic.

The fundamental experience of the lecture room is strongly axial, enclosed as one is by the gently curving ceiling and viewing as one does lantern slides projected against the end wall. A secondary experience is asymmetrical, entering and leaving through one corner and sensing the balance between the colonnade seen in sharp perspective on the left and the large niche in the distance on the right.

Visitors to the Sackler Museum may, on entering, proceed across the entrance hall to a striking information and sales desk, a white, multifaceted tube surrounding the receptionist (fig. 99). Beyond are two galleries, one a small space for exhibitions used in classroom teaching, the other a large, unarticulated room of two thousand square feet devoted to temporary exhibitions. Screens and movable partitions can divide the larger space in ways best suited to the material on display at the time.

In the left-hand corner of the lobby is a passenger elevator offering access to the galleries, offices, and seminar and storage rooms above. Stirling is especially gifted as a designer of rooms, but the quality of the smaller of these cannot even be suggested by photographs. He has combined a keen awareness that all spaces must be organized into functionally effective suites with his remarkable sensitivity to proportions and the appealing placement of doors and windows. The degree of variety achieved is astonishing: each of the five seemingly identical office floors has a different focus and a personality of its own. And throughout, one is aware of the architect's skill in exploiting exceptional volumes—the largest and the smallest seminar rooms, the mixture of one-story and two-story spaces within the same storage area, and especially the long library reading room, curving away from the entering viewer at its far end, all combine to create diversity among the suites. Appropriately so, for those who use them, whether staff, students, or professors, use them for long hours, day after day.

The future visitor may wish to enter at the top, via the bridge from the Fogg. This connector will have to be one hundred fifty feet long, and as Broadway is a major street it will be conspicuous. What cannot be hidden it is best to emphasize, and Stirling has planned a monumental structure (figs. 104, 105). In the center will be two circular windows, each thirteen feet in diameter, over the middle of the street, which passes diagonally beneath the bridge. Starting from the Fogg, the visitor will first enter a long narrow gallery reserved for the display of graphic works before reaching a lounge focused on the two circular windows overlooking Broadway. A further gallery housing Harvard's unique collection of Chinese jades will lead into the new museum.

Of all the suites of rooms within the Sackler, the most remarkable are the upper two floors of galleries intended for the display of the permanent collection (fig. 108). Decisive to their aesthetic character is the design of the ceilings and the method of admitting daylight in the top-floor galleries. The curatorial staff strongly preferred natural light to illumine the ancient and Oriental sculptures and bronzes exhibited on the top floor. They also wished to avoid skylights, which invariably allow water to trickle in and heat to leak out. Stirling's solution is light monitors four feet high and sixteen feet across raised over the center of the gallery ceiling (fig. 103). The outer walls are of glass; four feet in from these, a wall hangs down from the roof and, at the bottom, flares out toward the two parallel walls of the gallery. This acts as a reflector, concentrating the daylight along the gallery walls. A horizontal plane encloses the bottom of the reflectors and forms the center of the gallery ceiling. The sloping sections at the top of the walls not only serve to distribute the light but also enclose the heating and ventilation ducts.

The effect looking up at the ceiling is of a complex sculptural form containing two channels of bright light (fig. 108). It says much for the effectiveness of the monitors that even on the sunniest days these channels are not glaringly bright. In fact, the most remarkable feature of the interior of the museum is the variety and sophistication of its lighting—the exceptionally pleasant use of everyday opportunities, ingenious inventions, and theatrical effects.

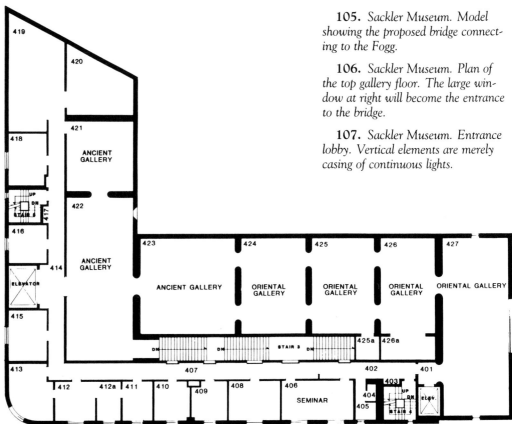

105. *Sackler Museum. Model showing the proposed bridge connecting to the Fogg.*

106. *Sackler Museum. Plan of the top gallery floor. The large window at right will become the entrance to the bridge.*

107. *Sackler Museum. Entrance lobby. Vertical elements are merely casing of continuous lights.*

The assertive top-floor ceiling is balanced by other strong details. For example the thick jambs of the doorways are half-cylinders of natural oak. Each jamb carries a slightly recessed lintel in the center of which is a small but noticeable circular opening for a security device. The wood of the jambs is matched by a kick plate one foot high, also of oak, that runs around the foot of the gallery walls and contains ventilating apertures. Stirling has also varied the sizes and axes of the galleries (fig. 106). The total effect, positive and formal, will surprise those who believe that a museum gallery should be as neutral as possible, a mere background for works of art. But most works of art were intended for rooms that were anything but neutral. Anyone who has displayed objects in spaces of positive architectural character knows how much this juxtaposition can add to the total effectiveness of the work of art.

The most dramatic sensation is reserved for last. Having admired the top-floor galleries, one turns to descend the stairs to the floors below and confronts an astonishing canyon, seven feet wide and fifty-one feet deep, brilliantly skylit (fig. 109). Here the striping of the exterior recurs, but in bands of yellow and lavender above the faintly greenish gray of the bluestone steps. On the right the lavender band is punctuated by windowlike openings that transmit the light of the stairwell into the corridors linking the offices (fig. 106). On the left a remarkable group of Coptic architectural fragments in low relief are set into the wall so that those looking out the corridor windows confront a piece of sculpture only seven feet away.

108. *Sackler Museum. Gallery of sculpture from classical antiquity.*

Midway down, a striking column, only partly visible in a large, dark niche, announces the entrance to the middle floor of galleries. It recalls the columns of the lecture hall, but half of it protrudes from the plane of the wall, and clearly this is a disengaged column. To the first-time visitor, the Sackler is nothing if not a building of positive statements. To the repeat visitor, the disengaged column on the stairway may be the first intimation that it is also a building of counterstatements, of quotations, even self-quotations, each one wryly made or used.

The second-floor galleries need not be described, for in form they resemble those above. However, being devoted to works of art with fugitive colors, the lighting is almost entirely artificial with the exception of a skylit bay opposite the gallery entrance. This holds a handsome group of Chinese rocks intended to bring a hint of natural forms into the spaces used for East Asian painting and decorative arts.

Proceeding further down, the contrast between the bright space of the upper stairwell and the relative darkness of its final flight becomes more marked, until the left-hand wall ceases and the eye travels across an open corridor to the welcome lightness of the entrance lobby. Turning back to survey what one has passed through, one sees a view quite as dramatic as that from above. The column now seems full and robust. In the intense light at the top all forms lose their precision and the violet of the walls melts into the blue of the sky. An unexpectedly witty touch is the head of the door at the top. This echoes the roof of the vestibule, a truncated triangular shape. But the sloping lines against the vertical plane resemble the lines of the side of the stairway as they converge in perspective. This is a hint that the glass door

might be a mere interruption. Does the stair really climb further—indeed, does it climb forever?

A final significant aspect of the Sackler Museum is its relation to the neighboring buildings (fig. 98). Daily, at rush hours, the short section of Quincy Street adjoining the museum carries two lanes of traffic, bumper to bumper. Stirling has set the facade of this building well back from this street, partly to line it up with the front of the Fogg but also to lessen the impact of the dense vehicular traffic passing by, and he has provided for an exceptionally broad brick sidewalk shaded by locust trees. Immediately north of the Sackler, across Cambridge Street, is the row of concrete columns that support the facade of Gund Hall, home of Harvard's Graduate School of Design. Stirling had the happy idea of aligning his locust trees with those columns and planting them the same distance apart.

In the immediate vicinity of the new building are an astonishing variety of structures: across Quincy Street, a neo-Georgian fire station of red brick with limestone trim (fig. 104); beyond, on the same side of Quincy Street, Memorial Hall, an enormous high-Victorian, cathedral-like structure, Gothic in style, flamboyant in manner; opposite this, just beyond the Sackler Museum on its side of Quincy Street, is the complex concrete Graduate School of Design, built in 1972 (fig. 98). In the background is William James Hall, a concrete skyscraper, junior grade; behind the new building is a simple red brick apartment house, and across Broadway the neo-Georgian Fogg. A basic concern of Stirling's has been to relate his design to its neighbors. Not only does the Sackler's rectangular entrance pavilion resemble the scale of the terminal unit of the Fogg, but the brick and stucco facade recalls the rusticated limestone entrances for the fire engines, likewise outlined against a brick wall. Stirling's bands on the walls echo the strongly colored stripes of Memorial Hall's slate roof and parody the strip windows of the School of Design and the mini-skyscraper.

Yet all these resemblances are minor touches. Neighbors will discover them gradually and get lasting pleasure from noting them. The first-time visitor will confront a strong, simple exterior, remarkably original but admirably coordinated. Within there are impressive public and pleasant private rooms. The functional relationships to one another are unusually intricate. Stirling's brilliant *parti* has produced a building at once striking, convenient, and—above all—a sympathetic setting for works of art.

109. *Sackler Museum. View from the top floor down the main stairway.*

Conclusion

One justification for these essays is the fact, already noted, that every leading twentieth-century architect has designed an art museum. Most of these designs, especially those actually executed, date from after World War II. The majority exemplify a new phase in twentieth-century architecture: a desire to create monuments. That phase was anticipated in an extraordinarily prescient manifesto written in 1943 jointly by José Luis Sert, Fernand Léger, and Sigfried Giedion.[1] There is no better approach to the buildings discussed above than to reprint most of their statements.

1. Monuments are human landmarks which men have created as symbols for their ideals, for their aims, and for their actions. They are intended to outlive the period which originated them, and constitute a heritage for future generations. As such, they form a link between the past and the future.

2. Monuments are the expression of man's highest cultural needs. They have to satisfy the eternal demand of the people for the translation of their collective force into symbols. The most vital monuments are those which express the feeling and thinking of this collective force—the people.

3. Every bygone period which shaped a real cultural life had the power and the capacity to create those symbols. Monuments are, therefore, only possible in periods in which a unifying consciousness and unifying culture exist. Periods which

exist for the moment have been unable to create lasting monuments.

4. The last hundred years have witnessed the devaluation of monumentality. . . . The so-called monuments of recent date, with rare exceptions, . . . in no way represent the spirit or the collective feeling of modern times.

5. This decline and misuse of monumentality is the principal reason why modern architects have deliberately disregarded the monument and revolted against it. . . . Today modern architects know that buildings cannot be conceived as isolated units, that they have to be incorporated into the vaster urban schemes. . . . Monuments should constitute the most powerful accents in these vast schemes.

6. A new step lies ahead. Postwar changes in the whole economic structure of nations may bring with them the organization of community life in the city which has been practically neglected up to date.

7. The people want the buildings that represent their social and community life to give more than functional fulfillment. They want their aspiration for monumentality, joy, pride and excitement to be satisfied. . . . A monument being the integration of the work of the planner, architect, painter, sculptor, and landscapist demands close collaboration between all of them. . . . As a rule, those who govern and ad-

minister a people, brilliant as they may be in their special fields, represent the average man of our period in their artistic judgments. . . . The feeling of those who govern and administer the countries is untrained and still imbued with the pseudo-ideals of the nineteenth century. This is the reason why they are not able to recognize the creative forces of our period. . . .

8. Sites for monuments must be planned. This will be possible once replanning is undertaken on a large scale which will create vast open spaces in the now decaying areas of our cities. In these open spaces, monumental architecture will find its appropriate setting. . . .

9. Modern materials and new techniques are at hand. . . . Mobile elements can constantly vary the aspect of the buildings. . . . Elements of nature, such as trees, plants, and water, would complete the picture. . . . Monumental architecture will be something more than strictly functional. It will have regained its lyrical value. In such monumental layouts, architecture and city planning could attain a new freedom and develop new creative possibilities, such as those that have begun to be felt in the last decades in the fields of painting, sculpture, music, and poetry.

Of the twelve museums discussed in this book, four—the Gardner, the Johnson sculpture gallery, Louisiana, and Huntington—show how different kinds or aspects of domestic architecture can be adapted to public use. They in no way seek to be monuments and are fundamentally unrelated to the issues raised in the manifesto. The remaining eight are to a greater or lesser degree monuments in terms of the manifesto, Beaubourg following it the most faithfully.[2] Indeed several of them are among the most important monuments erected since the war.[3]

There are at least two reasons for this widespread resemblance. Few of the trustees who control the building of art museums are close to the outlook of the average man. Some of them are likely to be more in sympathy with the most creative artists of our period than most of those who govern and administer the people. Potentially they are good clients for progressive architecture. Moreover, museums do represent social and community life and it has long been accepted that they should give more than functional fulfillment, that properly they must express the highest of aesthetic values.

Yet in every example discussed above there is one basic divergence from the manifesto. The ideals those writers considered are primarily ideals for exteriors—buildings as *symbols* for ideals—and are involved in planning, namely the relation of one building to another. The perfect monument for those writers was perhaps the Parthenon, visually a focus, the outcome of a remarkable collaboration between at the very least a ruler, a planner, an architect, and a sculptor. Significantly the word "interior" is not mentioned in the manifesto. The concept is not even implied.

The program and site of an art museum can be such that it becomes an expressive sculptural form, as at the Yale Center for

British Art. Alternatively the building can be integrated with other activities that together produce a significant exterior effect, as at Beaubourg. But the architectural theme of most of the buildings discussed above is a central courtyard surrounded by one or more levels of galleries. Exterior appearance is a secondary phenomenon.

In nineteenth-century museums the galleries referred (at least by implication) to a way of life, notably to living at a grand scale. The epitome of this attitude is the period room. Since the Depression the emphasis has been on viewing. In practice this means the proper lighting of works of art. The most varied experiments have been tried, from Mrs. Gardner's window-side table with small paintings at right angles to the light to Philip Johnson's calculated overhead mixture of daylight, shadow, and cathode tube illumination. Again this concentration on viewing has brought excellent results: witness the painting galleries at Yale and the provisions for the display of sculpture in the original building of the Museum of Modern Art, the Johnson gallery, Tokyo, and Louisiana.

Lighting aside, until quite recently the ideal has been an architecturally neutral gallery, one that is intended not to distract from the object by the prominent inclusion of any obtrusive structural or decorative elements. The space is meant to be equally accommodating to the greatest variety of works of art. The fact that most works of art were designed for an architectural environment that was anything but neutral has been ignored. The fact that certain ones can benefit enormously from an interplay with a positive background has been sacrificed to a consuming desire for flexibility. This means that almost any object can be

made to look reasonably well almost anywhere.

Another negative feature of contemporary gallery design has been the almost total disregard for visitors. "Confusing," "monotonous," "museum feet," those age-old complaints are still being voiced about the newest museums. Effectively curators are the clients for whom galleries are designed, and their wish is to have *their* objects look well in *their* galleries. They display little interest in who the visitors are and less in what they might want. Thus a recent analysis of attendance at one major American art museum showed that more than half the visitors came not singly but in groups of two or three. The most casual observation reveals that these people come together and wish to stay together, but their interest in a given object or group of objects varies greatly. Mother wants to relax while her college-age children argue about degrees of realism or discuss the condition of a painting. She wants to sit down; all too often she cannot; there are no seats nearby, for seats disturb the harmony of a curator's gallery.

Lobby-courts are generally not satisfactory for the exhibition of objects. The scale overwhelms works of art of usual size, as at the Gardner, or if large works are bought or commissioned for the area they are likely to look like pleasant decorative accessories, as at the East Wing. The most effective function of these central spaces is to establish a mood that will color the whole visit—be it majestic seriousness as at Berlin, the austerity of scholarly endeavor as in New Haven, or at least by implication "what a place for a party" (for instance at exhibition openings) as at the East Wing.

A more fruitful consideration is the specific relation of the court to the galleries. At the Museum of

Modern Art there was only a vast vestibule, linking entrance to elevators, galleries, and garden. At the Sackler it is reduced in extent, wholly devoted to a landing for multiple stairways, but monumental in height and diction. At the Gardner the court is such a splendor of flowers and architectural fragments that virtually all the galleries turn inward toward it. At Tokyo it sets a dedicated tone for the galleries. At the East Wing its impression is so powerful that the galleries seem afterthoughts. At Berlin the temporary exhibitions it contains would appear to be the whole museum; the important permanent collection is relegated to the basement. At the Guggenheim the court is as dominant as is the pavilion at Berlin and as much the focus as at the Gardner. At Johnson's sculpture gallery the center is well-nigh everything.

There is no mistaking the interior of an art museum. The combination of works of art and the galleries containing them is distinctive. The same cannot be said for their monumental exteriors. As has already been noted, the East Wing might be taken for a library, a hospital, or the headquarters of a bank.[4] The authors of the manifesto might have maintained that the fine arts have not yet become part of the collective force of the people. The appreciation of the fine arts is in one sense or another elitist, especially the appreciation of contemporary art. Eleven of the museums discussed have been involved with modern art, most of them exclusively so. But everybody concerned agrees that basic elitism must not be openly affirmed in buildings intended to serve the public. And so these abstractly monumental exteriors express nothing.

A sense of disappointment, as noted in the introduction, seems part of our response to these mu-

seums. Most of those discussed have been designed by our most admired architects. Several must have seemed like ideal opportunities—almost unlimited funds to spend, few restraints as regards site and space, widespread public support for the project, indeed enthusiasm. Why the all-but-universal disappointment?

It is perhaps constructive to consider which museums are the least unsuccessful as entities. Certainly the museums that were originally private collections fall into this category. In part this is because, usually, the architect was dealing with a collector and did not have to consider the varying demands of individual museum professionals; in part the owner's tight control of finances prevented the architect giving full rein to his spatial ambitions at the expense of the sympathetic display of the works of art.

What almost all other museums lack is coherence. This is because there is no professional agreement as to the proper relationship of the parts to one another. To visit a large museum is not like reading a history of art, but rather like perusing an encyclopedia of art history whose entries are arranged in a sequence incomprehensible to the reader. In most cases the organizing scheme adopted was determined by outdated or obscure local desiderata of one sort or another. The result is that most members of the public don't know what to expect and have few intelligent convictions as to what they want to see.

An initial orientation program is the solution currently in favor. Too many of these ignore the fact that people come to museums eager to see works of art, and to see them soon, not to look at slides and listen for half an hour to some faintly patronizing disquisition on the wonders in store.

Complementary is the failure of most museums easily to satisfy the visitor who does know what he wants to see. This is likely to be primarily a question of making conveniently available works of art that are not on exhibition. In the preceding pages little has been said of the way this obligation has been met because there is rarely anything decent, let alone significant to say.[5]

The contrast with public libraries is astounding. There are tens of millions of books in each of the greatest libraries in the world. In all large American libraries a few tens of thousands of reference works are freely available to all, in an easily accessible reading room. A public catalogue lists the institution's entire holdings, and generally arrangements can be made so that any local resident or visiting scholar can, after a short time, consult any volume he wishes.

The works of art owned by several of our largest museums may reach a figure like two or three million. The number exhibited at any one time might range from ten to twenty thousand. The inaccessibility of the remainder is scandalous. One can generally (albeit with difficulty) arrange to see a given object (if it is not still in a crate), only to find it abominably stored in an ill-lit, overcrowded basement. Not only is there no public catalogue, there is no general catalogue of any kind. One can discover all the works by Diderot in the research branch of the New York Public Library by spending perhaps an hour in one convenient place.[6] To discover how many works by Daumier the Metropolitan Museum owns, one must arrange by correspondence to consult four separate and private catalogues at the convenience of four different groups of the curatorial staff.[7] Nor does the discrepancy end here. There is nothing in the

American art world to compare with the system of branch public libraries that every American city maintains.

New art museums are greeted with great enthusiasm. Even when, as at Beaubourg, many people dislike the building, attendance increases mightily. Less evident is any widespread increase in depth of the visitors' comprehension. The conflict between the ideal of universal understanding of works of art and the fact of limited apprehension continues, and however faintly, however unjustly, the architecture is blamed. Yet it is hard to see how that basic situation can change until art becomes a more integral part of many people's lives. And that is not likely to happen as long as such a high proportion of the finest artistic achievements of the present and the past remain for all practical purposes invisible in the storerooms of a few of our largest museums.

To cure this deplorable situation requires a change in viewpoint. "Make great art easily, even casually visible" should be a widely accepted motto for our postmodern age.

The Humana building in Louisville, Kentucky, a corporate headquarters completed in 1986, presents an astonishing example of what can be accomplished. Here, in the lobby, dark green marble niches strikingly present a pair of splendid Greco-Roman statues to all who enter. Other works of art, large in scale, are destined for public spaces elsewhere in the building. Two imaginative business leaders, David Jones and Wendell Cherry (himself a collector), collaborated closely with the architect of their skyscraper, Michael Graves, to achieve this. May others, within and without the museum world, be inspired by their example.

Notes

Introduction

1. Pier Luigi Nervi might be supposed an exception. It is not generally remembered that he did make a design for a new building for the Pitt-Rivers Museum in Oxford. See *Architects' Journal* 147, no. 13 (March 1968): 639–642.

2. Philip C. Johnson, "Letter to the Museum Director," *Museum News* 38, no. 5 (Jan. 1960): 22.

3. In the middle 1970s both the Museum of Fine Arts, Boston, and the Metropolitan Museum in New York made detailed surveys of the people who visited them. Although public reference was made to the Metropolitan's survey, neither was published. Apparently there was no significant discussion of the implications for the museum program of the information they contained.

4. *The United States with an Excursion into Mexico*, ed. Karl Baedeker (Leipzig, 1893; rpt. New York: Da Capo Press, 1971), pp. 42–43, 80, 282.

Chapter I

1. The most complete bibliography is in an unpublished article, K. Orville, "The House That Jack Built," a copy of which I studied at the Gardner Museum. Certainly the briefest and perhaps the most balanced biography is George L. Watson, "Gardner, Isabella Stewart (Apr. 14, 1840—July 17, 1924)," in *Notable American Women: A Biographical Dictionary*, ed. Edward T. James, 3 vols. (Cambridge, Mass.: Belknap Press of Harvard University Press,

1971), 2:15–17. Morris Carter's *Isabella Stewart Gardner and Fenway Court* (Boston: Houghton Mifflin, 1925) was written by a contemporary who knew her well. Louise Hall Tharp's *Mrs. Jack* (Boston: Little, Brown, 1965) is the most widely informative.

2. The death of her son was followed by that of a sister-in-law to whom she was devoted. Then came a miscarriage, which almost cost her life and prevented further children. A Gardner nephew was named for her husband; he proved retarded. A Gardner brother-in-law died in 1875 leaving three orphan boys, the oldest in his early teens. She and her husband brought them up. The first-born committed suicide in his twenties, while the most intelligent withered into a pedantic recluse. Only one of the three "lived happily ever after." Meanwhile her sister and both her brothers had died, so that at forty-one she was the last of her generation of Stewarts. After the death of her mother, her father remarried; her stepmother proved unsympathetic. Mr. Gardner lived to be sixty-two; she outlived him by twenty-six years. During the last five of those years she was paralyzed, following a stroke, and was unable to walk.

3. Watson, "Gardner, Isabella Stewart," p. 15.

4. Lubov Keefer, *Music Angels: A Thousand Years of Patronage* (Baltimore: Keefer, 1976), p. 173.

5. After her death the trustees changed the official name of the institution to The Isabella Stewart Gardner Museum.

6. In a letter to Mrs. Gardner quoted in Carter, *Isabella Stewart Gardner and Fenway Court*, p. 220.

7. Quoted in Tharp, *Mrs. Jack*, p. 16.

8. Karl Baedeker, *London and Its Environs* (Leipzig, 1894), pp. 275f.

9. From the copy of Sears' unpublished diary in the Gardner Museum.

10. Carter, *Isabella Stewart Gardner and Fenway Court*, p. 162.

11. In a letter quoted in ibid., p. 216.

12. Cornelius C. Vermeule III, *Sculpture in the Isabella Stewart Gardner Museum* (Boston, 1977), p. 44.

13. Henry James, *The American Scene* (New York: Scribners, 1946), pp. 254f.

14. In addition to Johnson the group included Alfred Barr, Henry-Russell Hitchcock, Jr., Lincoln Kirstein, "Chick" Austin, John McAndrew, Agnes Mongan, John Walker, and Edward Warburg. Alexander Calder, their contemporary, was nearby at this time, at the Massachusetts Institute of Technology.

15. Johnson has recently added another building to his complex, a study, and "does not work in the sculpture museum any more." From this visitor's limited and jaundiced point of view, a pity; in this rarefied context a busy but seated figure was a delightful surprise.

16. John Morris Dixon, "Sculpture Under Glass," *Architectural Forum* 133, no. 5 (Dec. 1970): 24. Dixon calls attention to the practical ingenuities of the design. "Steel pipe was chosen for the rafters because it can be cut to odd lengths and adjusted in strength—for different spans—by varying its wall thickness. . . . The ridge beam has a pierced web, exposed to the exterior on one side, where there are electrically operated ventilating shutters, like those of a typical greenhouse. . . . There is no air conditioning. Unit heaters, suspended from the roof ridge, maintain a minimum temperature of 50 degrees F in midwinter."

17. The bibliography on Louisiana is extensive. The following four titles (in chronological order) were the most useful in preparing the present text: "Louisiana: A New Danish Museum," *Museums Journal* 60 (Dec. 1960): 222–228; *Louisiana: Humlebaek, Copenhagen, Denmark* (Copenhagen: n.p., c. 1978); *Louisiana: The Collection and Buildings* (Copenhagen: n.p., 1982); and Laurence Weschler, "Profiles: Louisiana in Denmark," *New Yorker* 58, no. 29 (Aug. 30, 1982): 36–61. (The text in the first three of these is by Knud W. Jensen.) The following magazines contain articles that are usefully descriptive, verbally or visually: *AIA Journal* 68, no. 10 (Sept. 1979): 81; *Architectural Forum* 110, no. 5 (May 1959): 249; *Arkitektur* 2, no. 5 (Oct. 1958): 145–166; *Connoisseur Yearbook 1962*, pp. 130–133; *Country Life* 156 (Aug. 1974): 490–491; *Deutsche Bauzeitung* 107 (Jan. 1973): 55–59; *Oeil* no. 58 (Oct. 1959): 54–59; *Progressive Architecture* 41, no. 17 (Dec. 1960): 122–127.

18. *Museums Journal* 60: 226, 228, 222, 225; *Louisiana: Humlebaek*, pp. 4, 6.

19. *Museums Journal* 60: 227.

20. *Louisiana: Humlebaek*, p. 4; *Louisiana: Collection and Buildings*, p. 2.

21. *Museums Journal* 60: 222.

22. *Louisiana: Collection and Buildings*, p. 3.

23. *Museums Journal* 60: 223. This is the same figure that the Museum of Modern Art drew on one day of its recent Picasso show. (See Paul Goldberger, "The New MoMA," *New York Times Magazine*, April 15, 1984, p. 37.)

24. *Museums Journal* 60:225.

25. *Louisiana: Collection and Buildings*, p. 2.

26. That sentence describes the sculpture garden as it existed before the building of the recent south wing. Although this destroyed most of the sculpture garden, photographs suggest that it remains as beautiful if not as extensive as before.

27. *Louisiana: Collection and Buildings*, p. 7.

28. *Museums Journal* 60:222, 226.

29. *Museums Journal* 60:228.

30. The bibliography on the Yale Center is not extensive, but it is distinguished. Six works are of prime importance: Paul Mellon, "Remarks at the New Haven County Bar Association Dinner, 16 May 1975," on receiving the Liberty Bell Award (unpublished; a xerox copy was generously provided by the Yale Center); Yale Center for British Art, *Selected Paintings, Drawings & Books*, with a foreword by Paul Mellon (New Haven: Yale University, 1977); Jules David Prown, *The Architecture of the Yale Center for British Art* (New Haven: Yale University, 1977); John Walker, *Self-Portrait with Donors: Confessions of an Art Collector* (Boston: Little, Brown, 1974), pp. 178–204; Vincent Scully, Jr., "Yale Center for British Art," *Architectural Record* 161, no. 7 (June 1977): 95–104; and William Jordy, "Art Centre, Yale University," *Architectural Review* 162 (July 1977): 37–44 (abridged in *Werk* 65 [May–June 1978]: 50–52).

31. Mellon, "Remarks," p. 2.

32. *Selected Paintings*, p. ix; Walker, *Self-Portrait*, p. 191.

33. *The British Art Center at Yale* (New Haven: Yale University, 1979), p. 3.

34. *Selected Paintings*, p. xii; Mellon, "Remarks," p. 15.

35. *Selected Paintings*, pp. xi–xii.

36. *Selected Paintings*, p. x.

37. Prown, *Architecture of the Yale Center*, p. 43.

38. Jules David Prown, personal communication.

39. Scully, "Yale Center for British Art," p. 103.

40. Ibid., p. 104.

41. Prown, *Architecture of the Yale Center*, pp. 8–9.

42. Scully, "Yale Center for British Art," p. 104.

43. Duncan Robinson, Director of the Yale Center, in a letter to the author of October 29, 1982.

Chapter II

1. Quoted in Milton Lomask, *Seed Money: The Guggenheim Story* (New York: Farrar, Straus, 1964), p. 196.

2. For the bibliography on The Solomon R. Guggenheim Museum see Robert L. Sweeney, *Frank Lloyd Wright: An Annotated Bibliography* (Los Angeles: Hennessey & Ingalls, 1978), which covers material through October 1977.

3. "Walter Gropius, zu unserer Publikation der Guggenheim Museum," *Baukunst und Werkform* 13, no. 3 (March 1960): 115.

4. William J. Hennessey, "Frank Lloyd Wright and the Guggenheim Museum: A New Perspective," *Arts* 52 (April 1978): 132, n. 32.

5. Editor's Page, *AIA Journal* 33, no. 1 (Jan. 1960): 124, signed "Jim."

6. "Frank Lloyd Wright's Sole Legacy to New York," *Interiors* 119, no. 5 (Dec. 1959): 174.

7. "The Guggenheim Museum," *American Architect and Building News* 218 (July 27, 1960): 107; Frank Lloyd Wright, letter to Solomon R. Guggenheim, August 14, 1946, quoted in *The Solomon R. Guggenheim Museum: Architect, Frank Lloyd Wright* (New York: Guggenheim Foundation and Horizon Press, 1960), pp. 16, 15, 16, 18.

8. *Guggenheim Museum*, 1960, p. 23; *American Architect and Building News* 218: 110, 102.

9. *Guggenheim Museum*, 1960, pp. 17, 18, 15, 17.

10. *Guggenheim Museum*, 1960, p. 20; James Johnson Sweeney, "Chambered Nautilus on Fifth Avenue," *Museum News* 38, no. 5 (Jan. 1960): 15.

11. *Guggenheim Museum*, 1960, pp. 16, 40.

12. *Guggenheim Museum*, 1960, pp. 17, 15, 16, 21.

13. The original hanging was designed to suit the preferences of the donor of the works of art. It has since been rehung and greatly improved.

14. The Guggenheim addition has been discussed in *Architecture* 74, no. 12 (Dec. 1985): 11; *Art in America* 75, no. 7 (July 1987): 14–19; *Art News* 84, no. 6 (Summer 1985): 14–16; and *Progressive Architecture* 68, no. 3 (March 1987): 40–43, among others. At the time of writing, construction of the revised addition was expected to begin in the latter half of 1988.

15. Le Corbusier and Pierre Jeanneret, *Oeuvre Complète*, vol. 1 (Zurich: H. Girsberger, 1937), "Mundaneum, 1929," pp. 190–194.

16. Ibid., vol. 3 (Zurich: H. Girsberger, 1939), "Centre d'esthétique, 1936," pp. 152–155, and vol. 7 (New York: Wittenborn, 1965), "Centre international d'art à Erlenbach, 1963," pp. 164–177.

17. The principal sources of information are *Oeuvre Complète*, vol. 7 (New York: Wittenborn, 1965), "National Museum of Western Art at Tokyo, 1957–1959," pp. 182–191; *Japan Architect* 34 (Aug. 1959): 35–50; *A Short Guide to the National Museum of Western Art* (Tokyo, 1960); *Guide to the National Museum of Western Art* (Tokyo, 1964); and *Masterpieces of the National Museum of Western Art, Tokyo* (Tokyo, 1983). I am most grateful to Mr. Haruo Arikawa, Curator at the National Museum of Western Art, for his kindness in reading my manuscript concerning his museum and for supplying me with appropriate copies from these three volumes.

18. *Japan Architect*, Aug. 1959, p. 35.

19. In addition, Matsukata's collection included "more than 8,000 pieces of Ukiyo-e prints which had formerly belonged to the Vever Collection. Later this Ukiyo-e collection was donated to the Imperial Household Ministry in 1943, and is presently preserved by the National Museum of Tokyo." *Masterpieces*, p. 88.

20. Junzo Sakakura, "The Opening of the National Museum of Western Art," *Japan Architect*, Aug. 1959, p. 36.

21. *Oeuvre Complète* 7: 182.

22. Sakakura, "Opening of the National Museum of Western Art," p. 36, and *Japan Architect* 34 (June 1959).

23. An auditorium, far simpler than the one Le Corbusier designed, was completed at one side in 1964. It accommodates 262 people. A new wing at the rear, designed by Kunio Mayekawa, was opened in 1979. Here are displayed the works of western art that were not part of the original Matsukata collection.

24. "The *modulor* which Le Corbusier developed after many years of research is like a musical scale which gives order to the infinitude of possible musical pitches. Based on the size and proportions of the human body, it is a means of fitting architecture to the human spirit, of ordering the infinitude of possible proportions in such a way as to make them conform to the human shape. In the new Museum of Western Art, the *modulor* system has been observed in everything from the structural members to the architectural details and furnishings." (Tadayoshi Fujiki, *Japan Architect*, Aug. 1959, p. 48.)

25. "The contractors and workmen have done their work fastidiously—so much so that at times I wonder how Le Corbusier would feel about the smoothness of the finish. Being thoroughly acquainted with his ideas about the use of unfinished concrete, for example, I fear he will be disturbed to find the building lacking in the brute strength that characterizes

his usual work." (Sakakura, "Opening of the National Museum of Western Art," p. 36.)

26. Ibid.

27. The name of the institution was changed in 1987. "A Quiet Unobtrusive Building for the Contemplation of Art," *Architectural Record* 152, no. 1 (July 1972): 108f., is the only published article on this building that I know. Additional sources are the Huntington Galleries Biennial Reports for 1979–1981 and 1981–1983. The Architects Collaborative, through the kindness of Mr. Malcolm Ticknor, have supplied me with a pamphlet, *Huntington Galleries Addition: Community*; a copy of a typewritten notice, "Huntington Galleries Addition"; and "Last Summer," a reproduction of a talk by Walter Gropius at the ground breaking. (This was printed but I do not know where or by whom.) I am deeply indebted to four people. Mr. Malcolm Ticknor of The Architects Collaborative, who was Gropius' associate-in-charge in the design and building of the extension to the Galleries, discussed his experiences frankly and at length. In addition he generously provided me with much useful written information and several invaluable photographs. Mrs. Louise Polan, Curator at the Huntington Galleries, assembled their documents about the building in preparation for my visit and extended me every courtesy and assistance during my stay. Mrs. Roberta Shimm Emerson, until recently the director of the Galleries, was a trustee at the time Gropius was called upon to design the extension. She talked to me frankly and most interestingly both about the whole process of building and about the way the institution has operated in the quarters Gropius created. Mr. Alex Booth, chairman of the building committee when the Galleries extension

was erected, told me in remarkable detail about his experiences. Especially valuable was his evaluation of the circumstances that determined several of the fundamental decisions the Trustees and Gropius made.

28. Biennial Report, 1981–1983, p. 2. Total attendance in 1982 was 151,318. Of these, 38,000 were school children from twenty-five counties in the immediate tri-state region. More significant, perhaps, half of the total number of visitors had come during seventeen summer and autumn weeks to see one temporary exhibition, "The Armand Hammer Collection: Five Centuries of Masterpieces." These figures become even more astonishing when considered against the local population. In the 1950s, when the institution was founded, Huntington had a population of some 80,000, diminishing to 62,000 in 1984. The metropolitan area has held its own at 350,000 during these years. Only 17 1/2% of the Galleries' income derives from endowments, the remainder coming from admissions, tuition, memberships, grants, donations, and gifts.

29. After seventeen years of growth the museum is once again overcrowded, conspicuously so as regards that ever-neglected problem, proper storage of the collections. Only one relatively small area of the plateau remains for possible expansion (fig. 54). The alternatives are to create a separate building on another part of the site, some seventy-five feet below, or to build an additional floor over at least a part of the existing building. This would not only drastically alter its appearance, but would be visually unacceptable in the local environment.

30. The collections contain several diverse groups of excellent

objects but few masterpieces. The exhibition policy of the Galleries is admirable, but theoretically it should be complemented with extensive study-storage areas, where the visitor with a particular interest can examine, under good conditions, works of art not currently on display. At the moment this is not a pressing problem because the Huntington Galleries is too little known outside its tri-state area.

31. The original building cost $400,000. The trustees were unable to raise more than $300,000. They spent many depressing years struggling to pay off a mortgage.

32. At least subconsciously, Marshall College in Huntington may have resented the competition another cultural institution would provide. If there was to be a museum, it should be downtown and nearby. Even the school board was opposed. It was a great victory for the institution when the school board was persuaded to bring school classes to the museum by bus.

33. The completion of the new building brought about an astonishing increase in activities and services. To cite only a few simple statistics, in 1967 before the new building was started there were only 476 members, and an attendance of 35,000. In June 1983 there was a membership of 3,093, and attendance during the preceding year had been 151,000. This growth was made possible by applying for and receiving all possible grants. The amount available has now declined. To meet this drop the museum has embarked on a campaign to raise two million dollars in new endowments.

34. Walter Gropius, "Designing Museum Buildings," in his *Apollo in the Democracy: The Cultural Obligation of the Architect* (New York: McGraw-Hill, 1968), pp. 142–

150. Reprinted by permission of McGraw-Hill Publishing Company.

35. *Huntington Galleries Addition: Community*, column 1.

36. "Last Summer," n.p.

37. Almost more revealing than what Gropius demonstrated is what (perhaps reluctantly) he left alone. To repeat: "The various departments of a museum should be laid out as large neutral spaces enclosed by a permanent shell. . . . Rigidity of arrangement should be avoided for all departments." It would be hard to find a more complete disregard of those principles than the tangle of tight little rooms that from the beginning have constituted the administrative quarters at Huntington (figs. 53, 54).

38. Everybody at the Huntington Galleries' favorite quotation. Widely experienced as he was, Gropius never had to balance the budget of an American art museum.

39. Alex Booth, chairman of the building committee, stressed the satisfaction of working with Gropius. In Huntington, downriver from Pittsburgh, the normal support for monumental buildings is steel. Gropius specified concrete. The experienced but overconfident contractor had difficulty finding enough workmen skilled in using that material. This resulted, among other problems, in cobwebbing the concrete. Much had to be repaired or done over, to the contractor's great cost. But Gropius was insistent, and well done it was in the end. As construction advanced, both the contractor and the chairman of the building committee became worried by the absence of expansion joints in the immensely heavy concrete roof. Gropius' response over the telephone was "with as much mass as that, you don't need them," and right he was.

40. The one significant change in the plan the trustees persuaded Gropius to make was to place the stage of the auditorium at the outer instead of the inner end of its wing. The side entrance leading into the auditorium is therefore a secondary one. The main access is from inside the building. This means the foyer is more frequently and effectively used. Also musicians practicing disturb the museum less. The one disadvantage is that it is not possible to open the auditorium at night without keeping the museum open, but this would matter more in a large museum than in a small one. The present staff emphatically emphasize the virtues of using events in the auditorium to bring people into the museum.

41. According to Gropius, the half-barrel vaults derived from the Tate Gallery in London (*Apollo in the Democracy*, p. 146).

42. I am especially grateful to Mrs. Emerson for pointing out this shortcoming.

43. The principal descriptions of the National Gallery in Berlin are in *Architectural Design* 39 (Feb. 1969): 79–90; *Architectural Forum* 129, no. 3 (Oct. 1968): 34–47; *Architectural Record* 144, no. 5 (Nov. 1968): 115–122; *Architectural Review* 144 (Dec. 1968): 408–414; *Art Journal* 29, no. 1 (Fall 1969): 92–93; *Bauwerk* 59 (Sept. 1968): 1209–1226; *Deutsche Bauzeitung* 70 (June 1965): 476–477; Peter Carter, *Mies van der Rohe at Work* (New York: Praeger, 1974), pp. 94–98; *Domus* no. 478 (Sept. 1969): 1–6; *Pantheon* 27 (May 1969): 243–245; *Progressive Architecture* 49, no. 11 (Nov. 1968): 108–113; Peter Serenyi, "Spinoza, Hegel, and Mies: The Meaning of the New National Gallery in Berlin," *Journal of the Society of Architec-*

tural Historians 30 (Oct. 1970): 240; and *Werk* 56 (May 1969): 330–342.

44. *Architectural Review* 144:410.

45. I am obliged to Dr. Lucius Grisebach of the National Gallery who courteously explained in a letter a complex subject that is frequently misrepresented.

46. *Architectural Design* 39:79–90.

47. Carter, *Mies at Work*, p. 96.

48. Serenyi, "Spinoza, Hegel, and Mies," p. 240; *Pantheon*, p. 8.

49. James Johnson Sweeney, "Mies van der Rohe, 1886–1969," *Architectural Review* 146 (Dec. 1969): 480.

50. *Architectural Forum* 78, no. 5 (May 1943): 84–85; see also Franz Schulze, *Mies van der Rohe: A Critical Biography* (Chicago: University of Chicago Press, 1985), p. 230.

51. "The inaugural exhibition of Mondrian was not discussed with Mies. He even protested, because he found that opening his building with a Mondrian show would once again support a very common misunderstanding that his architecture had anything to do with the philosophy of 'de stijl' or constructivism. Mies preferred to be linked with Schinkel and his classicist tradition." Letter to the author from Dr. Lucius Grisebach.

52. Ibid. Ultimately the city expects to have a museum devoted entirely to temporary exhibitions. What will the upper floor of the National Gallery be used for then?

53. "Mies, quoted in 'Mies van der Rohe,' film directed by Georgia van der Rohe." As repeated in Schulze, *Mies: A Critical Biography*, p. 309.

Chapter III

1. This account of the building of the museum is largely dependent upon Russell Lynes, *Good Old Modern: An Intimate Portrait of the Museum of Modern Art* (New York: Atheneum, 1973), especially chapter XI, "Home Is Where You Hang Your Collection." Also important is A. Conger Goodyear (the first chairman of the board), *The Museum of Modern Art: The First Ten Years* (New York, 1943). I read much of the large body of reporting, interpretation, and criticism in contemporary newspapers and periodicals, but it provided no information not found in the above sources, nor opinions of remarkable interest.

2. Robert A. M. Stern, *George Howe: Toward a Modern American Architecture* (New Haven: Yale University Press, 1975), pp. 104–106.

3. In the late nineteenth century certain wealthy New York families bought up pieces of real estate near one another on which to build houses for their families. The best-known instance is the Vanderbilts, who created a series of houses along Fifth Avenue at the corners of 51st, 52nd, and 57th Streets. The Rockefellers owned several house lots on streets in the low fifties west of Fifth Avenue. It is perhaps no accident that Rockefeller Center was developed likewise west of Fifth Avenue a short distance to the south, although the Rockefellers did not own the property on which it stands.

4. Goodyear, *The First Ten Years*, pp. 15f. The quotation is from the museum's charter.

5. The Museum of Modern Art does not, to my knowledge, publish annually the figures of its operating expenses and receipts. Because of its relatively few galleries, and these relatively modest, few people realize that in terms of annual operating expenditure it is one of the largest museums in the country—some years, perhaps, being the second or third largest. Those facts are vividly reflected in the balance of the staff.

6. The Museum of Modern Art was one of the first in this country to seek energetically to develop a large membership. Access to the top floor was one privilege of membership, as was a substantial reduction in the price of the excellent publications that at Alfred Barr's insistence the Museum has produced from the beginning. Some figures suggest that at least in earlier years the number of members varied markedly from year to year according to the number of publications being produced.

7. The street was not extended because Restaurant 21 refused to sell their site. Goodyear, *The First Ten Years*, p. 21.

8. Lynes, *Good Old Modern*, p. 193.

9. Stern, *George Howe*, p. 106, n. 45.

10. For the addition to the Museum of Modern Art see Stanley Abercrombie, "MoMA Builds Again," *Architecture* 73, no. 10 (Oct. 1984): 87–95 (quotation, p. 94); Mildred F. Schmertz, "Modern Architecture for Modern Art," *Architectural Record* 172, no. 2 (Oct. 1984): 164–177; and Paul Goldberger, "The New MoMA," *New York Times Magazine*, April 15, 1984, pp. 37ff.

11. Mr. Carter Brown, Director of the National Gallery, has kindly informed me that House Resolution 217, 75th Congress, approved March 24, 1937, established the Gallery and reserved the site for future expansion. In the 1930s the site of the East Wing had been used for a Public Works project; later there were tennis courts here. See Suzanne Slesin, "Washington's Newest Monument: The Man Who Designed It," *Esquire* 89, no. 10 (June 6, 1978): 33f.

12. Originally the National Gallery acquired only works of art by artists who had been dead for several decades. With the acquisition of the Chester Dale Collection in 1962, this policy was changed and the Gallery began acquiring works by established living artists. Indeed several such works were commissioned to adorn the East Wing.

Only quite recently has the Museum seriously concerned itself with problems of conservation.

13. The original project for a study center was also to have included a small museum. ("Flexibility for a Changing Role at National Gallery Addition," *Industrial Design* 27 [Jan. 1980]: 47.)

14. Andrew Mellon left the National Gallery 126 paintings and twenty-six pieces of sculpture. By the 1970s the collection contained some 30,000 works of art. (Benjamin Forgey, "An Exhilarating Triumph in Washington," *Art News* 77, no. 6 [Summer 1978]: 59; David W. Scott, "Plans and Programs—The National Gallery East Wing," *Connoisseur* 178 [Dec. 1971]: 264.) Of these, approximately 25,000 are prints in the Rosenwald Collection.

15. Figures concerning the National Gallery are easy to come by, but do not always agree. The total area, East and West Wings, is almost one million square feet (Lori Simmons Zelenko, "An Interview with J. Carter Brown," *American Artist* 45 [May 1981]: 85). The

area under the plaza contains 150,000 square feet, the East Wing 450,000, of which 110,000 is exhibition space ("National Gallery New Wing Opens," *Progressive Architecture* 59, no. 5 [May 1978]: 25).

16. "Museums: Pei's 'Splendid Solution' for the National Gallery," *Interiors* 130, no. 11 (June 1971): 18; "I. M. Pei: On Museum Architecture" (interview), *Museum News* 51, no. 1 (Sept. 1972): 14.

17. It is said that Pei hit on the idea of subdividing the trapezoid into two triangles while returning from Washington to New York on the plane and sketched it on the spot (Werner Oechslin, "Pei's Neubau der National Gallery in Washington," *Werk* 66 [Jan. 1979]: 33). Reproductions of Pei's sketches are found in Slesin, "Washington's Newest Monument," p. 33, and Barbaralee Diamonstein, "I. M. Pei: 'The Modern Movement Is Now Wide Open,'" *Art News* 77, no. 6 (Summer 1978): 66.

18. For the concept of the study center see J. Carter Brown, "What Is to Become of the National Gallery of Art," *Connoisseur* 178 (Dec. 1971): 259–262. For the completed building see Andrea O. Dean, "Visual Arts Study Center Opens in Second East Building Triangle," *AIA Journal* 69, no. 2 (Oct. 1980): 16.

19. "Museum-going is not just an aesthetic and educational experience, but a form of recreation as well. . . . We have to design spaces large enough to accommodate large crowds." ("I. M. Pei: On Museum Architecture," p. 14.)

20. "Flexibility for a Changing Role at National Gallery Addition," *Industrial Design* 27 (Jan. 1980): 47; Donald Canty, "Building as Event," *AIA Journal* 68, no. 6 (Mid-May 1979): 112.

21. "The real mystery of Mr. Pei's palace is why does it learn so little from its great neighbour? Russell Pope's classical revival National Gallery is one of the most agreeable art galleries in the world. . . . The domed central space and two garden courts are reached at just the right moment when the visitor wants to rest." (Colin Amery, "Inside the NGA," *Architectural Review* 165 [Jan. 1979]: 22.) "A strong impression prevails that the galleries were not thought to need the quality of architectural care that obviously was given to the concourse." (William Allen, ibid., p. 30.)

22. *Industrial Design* 27:47.

23. Amery, "Inside the NGA," p. 22.

24. This statement is not strictly true. As Mr. Carter Brown has helpfully pointed out, in the southwestern portion of the West Wing the galleries are finished in a variety of materials and colors, velvet, damask, oak, and limestone, but by the time one has reached them, or left the building, the memory of monotony is dominant. Amery declares of these same galleries in a classic of faint praise, "The arrangement of small and larger rooms off the main corridors is easy on the feet and on the eyes" ("Inside the NGA," p. 22).

25. As was expected of him, Pei used the same quarries that had supplied the marble for the original building. He likewise graded the stone from dark at the bottom to light at the top, but was unable to achieve the delicate transitions of the original since some of the veins used then were now exhausted. (*Progressive Architecture* 55, no. 9 [Sept. 1974]: 92.)

26. Oechslin, "Pei's Neubau," p. 34. Pei comments on the regulations governing the entrance in *Architectural Record* 164, no. 2 (Aug. 1978): 82.

27. Oechslin, "Pei's Neubau," p. 34. This was by no means a new line of criticism. In 1842, Victor Hugo had written: "If it is right that the architecture of an edifice be adapted to its purpose in such a way that the purpose be readable from the edifice's exterior alone, we can never be sufficiently amazed at a monument which can equally well be a royal palace, a house of commons, a town hall, a college, a riding school, an academy, an entrepôt, a tribunal, a museum, a barracks, a sepulchre, a temple, a theatre. For the time being it is a Stock Exchange." (*Notre-Dame de Paris*, as quoted in T. J. Clark, *The Painting of Modern Life* [New York: Alfred A. Knopf, 1985], p. 32.)

28. Reyner Banham, "Enigma of the rue du Renard," *Architectural Review* 161 (May 1977): 277.

29. Two notable exceptions are Calvin Tomkins, "Profiles: A Good Monster," *New Yorker* 53, no. 48 (Jan. 16, 1978): 37–67, ostensibly a profile of Pontus Hulten, in fact an excellent account of the entire project, but without illustrations; and "Beaubourg Preview: An Interview with Pontus Hulten by Elizabeth C. Baker," *Art in America* 65, no. 1 (Jan.–Feb. 1977): 100–102.
The quantity of European writing about Beaubourg is daunting. For articles consult *Art Index*, vols. 20–29 inclusive, and the Royal Institute for British Architecture's *Annual Review of Periodical Articles* 7 (1971–72) and *Architectural Periodicals Index* 1–10 (1971–82). For books there are bibliographies in *Architecture d'Aujourdhui* no. 189 (Feb. 1977): 45 and *Museum*

(Unesco) 30, no. 2 (1978): 87, although few of the books there listed are readily available in this country. I have found the following especially useful: "Le Défi de Beaubourg," *Architecture d'Aujourdhui* no. 189 (Feb. 1977): 40–79; *Domus* nos. 503, 511, 558, 566; *Architectural Review* 161 (May 1977): 270–294; *Architectural Design* 47, no. 2 (1977): 86–151; *Techniques et Architecture* 34, no. 3 (Feb. 1972); *Arc* no. 63; *Crée* 46 (Jan.–Feb. 1977); Claude Mollard, *Le Centre National d'Art et de Culture Georges Pompidou* (Lyon: Deswarte-Garnier, 1975); Marie Leroy, *Le Phénomène Beaubourg* (Paris: Syros, 1977); Charles Debbasch, *La France de Pompidou* (Paris: Presses universitaires de France, 1974); Georges Pompidou, *Entretiens et discours, 1968–1974* (Paris: Plon, 1975); and the Pompidou Center's *Rapport d'activité* for 1978 and following years.

30. *Architectural Review* 161:272.

31. Georges Chambaz, "A propos du Centre National Georges Pompidou," *Arc* no. 63:27; Andrew Rabeneck, "Beaubourg: Process and Purposes," *Architectural Design* 47, no. 2:104; Georges Fradier, "The Georges Pompidou National Centre for Art and Culture, Paris," *Museum* (Unesco) 30, no. 2 (1978): 77.

32. *Architecture d'Aujourdhui* no. 189:80.

33. Ibid.; Debbasch, *France de Pompidou*, p. 261. The quotation is by the interim Minister of Cultural Affairs, M. Bettincourt, addressing the National Assembly during the budgetary debate of 1971.

34. Fradier, "Pompidou National Centre," p. 77; Georges Pompidou, "Declarations on Art and Architecture," gathered by the newspaper *Le Monde*, Oct. 17, 1972.

35. For accounts of these various concerns see respectively *Techniques et Architecture* 34, no. 3:40 and Martin Even, "Un Etat sans histoire," *Arc* no. 63:20; Bernard Pingaud, "Un Choix culturel," *Arc* no. 63:22 and Leroy, *Phénomène Beaubourg*, p. 56; Jean and Marie Eiffel, "Beaubourg: Innovations to a Trojan Horse," *Architectural Design* 47, no. 2:138 and Norma Evenson, *Paris: A Century of Change, 1878–1978* (New Haven: Yale University Press, 1979), pp. 301–309; and Chambaz, "A propos du Centre National," p. 26.

36. It would be difficult to exaggerate the degree to which senior French politicians concerned themselves with Beaubourg. Pompidou, the president, and Chirac, the prime minister, visited the site about every three months. Architect Richard Rogers has written: "Perhaps the greatest setback of all was the untimely death [in 1974] of President Pompidou, and the ensuing reduction of motivation and funds which affected the quality of finishes, maintenance and operation of the Centre." (Richard Rogers, *Richard Rogers & Architects*, ed. Barbie Campbell Cole and Ruth Elias Rogers [London: Academy Editions; New York: St. Martin's Press, 1985], p. 12.) Afterwards the minister of culture, Michel Guy, "tried to cut the project down to size. The election of Giscard, with his somewhat aristocratic, Louis-Quinze image, sowed panic in the ranks of the team that ran the Centre. But they counterattacked, led by Mme Pompidou—who enlisted Jacques Chirac. Michel Guy was pushed out." "Mme Pompidou, from now on, was on the watch. There she was, on the job, with her advisers of Elysée days. She looked over acquisitions, and sent a personal letter of thanks, on her husband's behalf, to all the recent donors of modern paintings." ("Beaubourg: The Containing of Culture in France," *Studio International* 194, no. 1 [1978]: 29, 33; see also Pompidou, *Entretiens et discours*, pp. 190ff.) One of the architectural staff told me that when the basements were completed pairs of ventilators were installed around the edge of the property. They looked hideous and all Paris protested. The architects replied that it was the best solution they could find and indicated they would not take it amiss if the client asked other engineers to consider the problem and come up with a better solution. The president sold the ventilators to Tinguely for one franc, and pieces of them could easily be recognized on the playful monster ("Kokodrome") he constructed in the middle of the ground-floor forum. Meanwhile two other teams of ventilating experts were consulted and eventually agreed that the original proposition was the only feasible solution. So more ventilators were installed. Giscard insisted that these new ones must be painted white. François Mitterand has said he backed Beaubourg "from the beginning, for he knew it would be a people's building" (quoted in a letter from Richard Rogers to the author).

37. These were Pontus Hulten as director of the art museum, and, in the musical organization, Vonko Globokar in charge of instruments and voices, Luciano Berio of electro-acoustics, and Gerald Bennett of coordination. See Anne Rey, "Dans un puits d'ivoire," *Arc* no. 63:39.

38. Evenson, *Paris*, p. 213; Baker, "Beaubourg Preview," p. 101.

Îlot insalubre 1: in 1920 the area was part of the worst slum in Paris (Evenson, p. 213).

39. "It should be noted that although Paris has an elected city council, it has [then had] no mayor as senior executive officer. In terms of decision-making, for matters of urban planning and others, all decisions taken by the city council ultimately had to be approved by the Prefect and central government, its Council of Ministers and the President." (Eiffel and Eiffel, "Innovations to a Trojan Horse," p. 138.)

40. For contrasting views of the same phenomenon consider these quotations: "Following Pompidou's December 1969 announcement, a working party made up of representatives of future occupants of Beaubourg met regularly to define an outline program . . . with the help of François Lombard of the Ministry's Architectural Department." (Rabeneck, "Beaubourg: Process and Purposes," p. 106.) "Millions were swallowed up in studies, meetings, programs, trips abroad for experts in an attempt to flesh out this muddled intention, to fill up the empty hulk, rudderless for lack of consensus." (Leroy, *Phénomène Beaubourg*, p. 28.)

41. The competition brief has not been published. The best summary is *Architectural Design* 47, no. 2:97.

42. *Techniques et Architecture* 34, no. 3:41; Mollard, *Centre National Georges Pompidou*, p. 63; *Architectural Design* 47, no. 2:97 (quotation).

43. Basic to the concept of Beaubourg was the belief in the importance of creativity, as has been noted. Just how the institution would achieve this was never clear (see Pontus Hulten's remarks

in *Domus* no. 558 [May 1976]: 55). "Polyvalent" seems to mean not so much "multipurpose" as "equal in value for a number of purposes." It would not seem identical with "multi-valent" as discussed by Charles Jencks in *The Language of Post-Modern Architecture* (New York: Rizzoli, 1977), pp. 182ff.

44. Piano and Rogers are generally given all-but-exclusive credit for the building. In fact, as they have emphasized, it was very much a collaborative achievement, although no outsider now can fairly distribute credit. For a list of all the participants see *Domus* no. 566 (Jan. 1977): 58.

45. Rue St. Martin was the ancient central north-south highway through Paris, the *cardo*, as was said, of the original Roman settlement Lutetia. To some it seemed a kind of desecration to close it off from traffic on wheels, one more reason to decry Beaubourg. Such sentimentalists seem like strange allies for Beaubourg's principal opponents, the cultural conservatives of the political left wing. No stranger, perhaps, than the right-wing politicians who sponsored aesthetic radicals to create Beaubourg.

46. *Richard Rogers & Architects*, pp. 18f., 91.

47. Ibid., p. 91.

48. "To optimize accessibility, below-ground storage was to be minimized and books, paintings and sculpture were to be stored instead in specially designed high-level, suspended mobile mezzanines. Today there are only a few simplified mezzanines, but the existing structure is designed to support the extra weight." (Ibid., p. 12.)

49. For these features of the original proposal see *Architectural Review* 161:284; *Domus* no. 566:14; and *Architectural Design* 47, no. 2:90, 128.

50. This and the following quotations are from the General Exposé that the architects submitted to the jury with their designs (reprinted in *Domus* no. 503 [Oct. 1971]). The idea for the electronic screens on the facade developed out of the Spanish Pavilion at the World's Fair of 1937; see Catherine Blanton Freedberg, *The Spanish Pavilion at the World's Fair of 1937* (New York: Garland Publishing, 1987).

51. Pompidou, *Entretiens et discours*, p. 191; *Architecture d'Aujourdhui* no. 189:80.

52. These various difficulties are recorded in *Architectural Design* 47, no. 2:90, 106, 108, 131; Mollard, *Centre National Georges Pompidou*, p. 27; and especially *Domus* no. 566:11–12, 14.

53. Speed of execution was essential. Pompidou's term ran out in 1975; the project should be finished and in use some months before then if it was to exert any favorable effect on the elections. In the event, Pompidou died before the Center was completed.

"This lack of time was an enormous advantage because it kept us from going back on decisions too often." (Piano and Rogers in an interview, *Domus* no. 566:14.)

54. "Beaubourg: The Containing of Culture in France," p. 30. The authors offer no evidence in support of these statements, but though more bluntly expressed they reproduce the suggestions of everybody else who has considered this matter.

55. For an authoritative statement of proposals that were not realized, see *Richard Rogers & Architects*, p. 12.

56. The name is derived from the Bavarian engineer H. Gerber (1832–1912), who in 1866 obtained a patent on a cantilevered girder and in 1867 used some on a bridge over the Main at Hassfurt. The best-known example of their use is in the Firth of Forth bridge in Scotland.

57. "5,000 tons compression and 1,000 tons tension on two column lines." (*Richard Rogers & Associates*, p. 95.) Each column also has to withstand a bending moment of 18,000 ton-meters. For further engineering details see *Architectural Review* 161:284, 289; *Architectural Design* 47, no. 2:132.

58. It is important to remember that this effect is far different from the architects' original concept. They and their close associates realized this at the time the building was finished. "The facade itself becomes an activity container, a three-dimensional structural framework with people walking on it and looking down from it, a wide variety of items clipped to it, tents, seating and audio-visual screens etc." ("Piano and Rogers: A Statement," *Architectural Design* 47, no. 2:87.) "I do not think the building was conceived as a smooth monument. It was seen as an infinitely adaptable three-dimensional space enclosure held up by adjustable scaffolding acting also as huge information walls giving all the news, art and information to the city. A giant playframe for adults to perform on, where the event is more important than the object—the means rather than the end. I think that was the architecture. What Paris has got was the engineering." (Ted Happold, "Beaubourg: Architecture or Engineering?", Ibid., p. 132.)

59. "This is a building of profound craftsmanship, practically made piece by piece. Its craftsmanship is that of every prototype. However, the techniques and processes obviously belong to today's culture. Nothing in Beaubourg is casual; everything was designed with a meticulous approach." (Renzo Piano, quoted in *Richard Rogers & Architects*, p. 61.) "The fundamental concept is that this project was built according to a model of designing . . . which is non-architectural, but more closely resembles the design of objects." (Casare Casali interviewing the architects in *Domus* no. 566:15.) This statement is even more true of some of the parts than of the whole.

60. An attractively simple idea, but its execution must have involved not only innumerable minor adjustments of the design, but repeated persuasion of conventionally trained specialists in air conditioning, electricity, plumbing, and other collaborating experts that this was indeed the best solution. "I don't think that 'Heroic' is too strong a term to describe the persistence which must have been needed to organise the external service wall overlooking Rue du Renard and to thread all those bits and pieces in and out of the building." (Dennis Crompton, "Centre Pompidou: A Live Centre of Information," *Architectural Design* 47, no. 2:110.)

61. The reactions of the left are recorded in Chambaz, "A propos du Centre National," p. 26; the quotation is from Pingaud, "Un Choix culturel," p. 19.

62. Leroy, *Phénomène Beaubourg*, p. 57.

63. "EB [Elizabeth Baker]: So you think this big centralization is in fact good. PH [Pontus Hulten]: Oh, I definitely think so. . . . You cannot have one Matisse in a hundred museums, that's silly. You have to have a central point. Of course, centralization can be a dangerous thing. But I think in this specific situation, as of now, it's something Europe hasn't had. And that it can be good." (Baker, "Beaubourg Preview," p. 102.) "A museum which truly displays 20th century art in its many media at Beaubourg is the answer to an essential need . . . but it arouses criticism: the centralization of culture in Paris, an excessive bureaucracy, the forgetting of regional needs." (*Arc* no. 63:2.)

64. Cost figures are not hard to find, but the discrepancies are considerable. Add to this the substantial variation in the value of the franc against the dollar. The figure of $100,000,000 as the cost of construction was decisively stated by Richard Rogers in a letter to the author. Some other estimates are higher. (See Leroy, *Phénomène Beaubourg*, pp. 118, 119; but cf. *Architectural Design* 47, no. 2:108, Pingaud, "Un Choix culturel," p. 22, "Beaubourg: The Containing of Culture in France," p. 33, and Baker, "Beaubourg Preview," p. 100.)

65. See Leroy, *Phénomène Beaubourg*, p. 54, and "Beaubourg: The Containing of Culture in France," pp. 34f.

66. Even, "Un Etat sans histoire," pp. 20f.; "Beaubourg: The Containing of Culture in France," p. 29 (quotation); Mollard, *Centre National Georges Pompidou*, p. 111.

67. "Beaubourg: The Containing of Culture in France," pp. 31f.

68. Quoted by Erick Steingraber in *Pantheon* 35 (April–June 1977): 165.

69. There is no overall discussion of the basements. The above paragraph is based on personal observation and an incidental reference by various writers. For the Institute of Acoustics and Music see Michael Davis, "IRCAM," *Architectural Design* 47, no. 2:134–137, and Anne Rey, "Dans un puits d'ivoire," and appropriate passages and drawings in the architectural journals cited above.

70. *Crée* 46 (Jan.–Feb. 1977): 26.

71. *Domus* no. 566:15. Compare Pei's remark to the journalists quoted above, p. 88.

72. Fradier, "Pompidou National Centre," pp. 81–84; *Domus* no. 566:12; *Architectural Design* 47, no. 2:100.

73. And 5,000 visitors at any one time (*Domus* no. 566:15). The supports for the floor were doubtless designed to be safe for a considerably larger number. "The load on the floors was fixed throughout at 500 kg" (Peter Rice and Lennart Grut, "Main Structural Framework of the Beaubourg Centre," *Acier. Stahl. Steel* [Sept. 1975], p. 303).

74. Forty-six percent of the visitors to the museum spent two hours there, and 27% three hours. (Pompidou Center, *Rapport d'activité*, 1978, p. 37.)

75. Fradier, "Pompidou National Centre," p. 81; Richard Rogers, letter to the author.

76. There is one major exception to this mode of presentation. At the northern end of the plaza, adjacent to the main building, is a modest, one-story structure intended to be a replica of Brancusi's studio. In this are displayed the contents of the original, which he bequeathed to the nation on the condition they be so displayed. Some say it is not exactly correct, although a casual glance at photographs of the original suggests it is at least nearly so.

At first sight, the crowd of sculpture seems arranged entirely casually, as one would expect. Gradually one perceives subtle contrasts, careful juxtapositions; a calculated display, his display. Perhaps this was not a good idea. But it was Brancusi's idea, and as such should tell us much about himself and his work. Perhaps, after repeated visits, one will manage to overlook the glibness and can evaluate the Brancusi studio for what it is, perhaps the largest and certainly the most personal one-man show of one of the greatest twentieth-century artists. Certainly it does represent the only radical break with the way Beaubourg's permanent collection is presented, and as such it raises many challenging and fundamental questions.

77. For the remodeling of the Musée National d'Art Moderne see *Connaissance des Arts* no. 387 (May 1984): 34, and no. 406 (Dec. 1986): 39; *Casabella* 49 (July–Aug. 1985): 54–63; *Architectural Review* 178 (Nov. 1985): 86–90; *Architecture d'Aujourdhui* no. 240 (Sept. 1985): 26–31; *Art in America* 73, no. 10 (Oct. 1985): 110–117; *AIA Journal* 72, no. 11 (Sept. 1983): 62–71; *Studio International* 196, no. 1003 (1983): 12–15; *Pantheon* 41 (June 1983): 173–174.

78. Paraphrased from a letter of Richard Rogers to the author.

79. Pompidou, *Entretiens et discours*, p. 195.

80. *Architectural Design* 47, no. 2:141.

81. "The Pompidolium," *Architectural Review* 161 (May 1977): 271, 277; "Centre Georges Pompidou," *Architectural Design* 47, no. 2:102.

82. In a marginal note on the manuscript of this essay. In a recent public lecture at Harvard University Stirling remarked: "The architect must look backward to move forward."

James Stirling, Michael Wilford and Associates, *James Stirling: Buildings and Projects* (New York: Rizzoli, 1985), pp. 339f., contains an almost complete bibliography of the Sackler Museum from 1979 to 1983. In addition to the items listed there, there are *James Stirling's Design to Expand the Fogg Museum: A Portfolio of Drawings* (Cambridge, Mass., 1981); "The Stirling Approach to Bridging the Old and the New," *GSD News* (Harvard University), Nov.–Dec. 1983, p. 7; David Joselit, "The Sackler Museum," *Art New England*, March 1983; Gary Wolf, "Stirling: Fogg," *Architectural Review* 175 (April 1984): 35–42; Martin Filler, "The Stirling Standard," *House and Garden* 157, no. 5 (May 1985): 170–181; and *The Arthur M. Sackler Museum, Harvard University* (Cambridge, Mass., 1985).

I am deeply grateful to Seymour Slive, John Rosenfield, and Leoni Gordon, who read these pages in manuscript and contributed many helpful suggestions.

83. Of two examples I have seen, one was printed on the back of a communication bearing the letterhead "Yale University" (where Stirling was teaching at the time) and the other on the back of a communication bearing the letterhead "Harvard University."

Conclusion

1. "Nine Points on Monumentality," reprinted in Sigfried Giedion's *Architecture, You and Me: The Diary of a Development* (Cambridge: Harvard University Press, 1958), pp. 48–51. Reprinted here by permission of Harvard University Press.

2. Reyner Banham called attention to the relation of Beaubourg to this manifesto in "Enigma of the rue du Renard," *Architectural Review* 161 (May 1977): 277. For the close relation of the manifesto to the Spanish Pavilion at the Paris World's Fair of 1937, see Catherine Blanton Freedberg, *The Spanish Pavilion at the Paris World's Fair of 1937* (New York: Garland Publishing, 1987). Obviously the linking intelligence was Sert's.

3. Notably Yale, the Guggenheim, Berlin, and the large interiors of the East Wing and Beaubourg. Divergences from the manifesto are equally striking. The plans of the Guggenheim were drawn before the site was chosen. In the words of that document, "It could be crammed in upon any old lot in any district." It is hard to think that this most stimulatingly eccentric of buildings in any way exemplified or seeks to exemplify the thinking and feeling of "the people," but Wright defended the design specifically because it was "democratic." The Museum of Modern Art was monumental in that it was planned to be the terminal focus of a street, one of two such in Radio City, but one of the few such in New York.

4. Werner Oechslin in *Werk* 66 (Jan. 1979): 34. A responsible and informed critic made almost identical comments about Beaubourg. I am unable to recover this reference.

5. The exceptions are creations of private collectors: Philip Johnson's sculpture gallery and Paul Mellon's Yale Center. The extensive study-storage of painting collections was initiated in Brooklyn, taken up at the National Gallery in London, and perfected at New Haven. In general, print collections have been the best stored. The arrangements for study and storing of rare books, illustrated books, prints, and drawings at Yale are excellent. In general the decorative arts are the worst stored, with sculpture a close second. I do not believe the Yale Center contains many works of sculpture or the decorative arts. Now that the collections have been fully transferred from the Fogg, the Sackler has extensive holdings in the art of antiquity and of the Orient. The storage has proved first-rate, especially for graduate students working in these fields.

6. Wolfgang Freitag, librarian of the Fine Arts Library at Harvard, pointed out in a personal memorandum to me that there are also "Union Catalogues in printed formats or in microfiche versions that link the holdings of an entire national library system, or several regional systems can be consulted in every major library, extending the scope of the individual institution. Entries are established according to internationally agreed-upon standards. For the past fifteen years cataloguing records generated by the principal research libraries have been produced in machine-readable form, which means that they can be easily distributed (and consulted) worldwide. Universal availability of bibliographical information, the joint goal of UNESCO and IFLA (International Federation of Library Associations), is going to be fully realized in the near future, thanks to electronics and networking."

7. In 1969 a Museum Computer Network was started but developed only slowly. Now the Getty Trust's Information program has taken over its efforts.

Photography Credits

Figures 1-11 were generously contributed by the Isabella Stewart Gardner Museum, Boston.

Figure 12 is reprinted from *Architectural Forum* 133, no. 5 (December 1970): 23.

Figure 13 was generously contributed by Philip Johnson.

Figures 14 and 15 were generously contributed by Harvard University (photographs by Harvard graduate students).

Figures 16–18, 21, 23, and 24 were generously contributed by the Louisiana Museum, Humlebaek, Denmark.

Figure 20 is reprinted from *l'Oeil* no. 58 (October 1959): 56, by permission of l'Oeil, revue d'art. Copyright 1959 l'Oeil, revue d'art.

Figures 19 and 22 are reprinted from *Arkitektura* 2, no. 5 (October 1958): 157, 158, by permission of Arkitektens Forlag, Copenhagen.

Figure 25 is reprinted from *Architectural Record* 161, no. 7 (June 1977): 95, by permission of Architectural Record.

Figures 26, 27, 31–35, and 37 were generously contributed by the Yale Center for British Art, New Haven, Connecticut (figure 26: photograph by Tom Brown; figures 31 and 37: photographs by Joseph Szaszfai).

Figures 28–30 were generously contributed by Marshall D. Myers. Copyright 1977 P/M.

Figure 36 was generously contributed by Jules David Prown.

Figures 38–43 were generously contributed by the Solomon R. Guggenheim Museum, New York (figures 39, 42, 43: photographs by Robert E. Mates).

Figures 44–46 are reprinted from Le Corbusier and Pierre Jean-neret, *Oeuvre Complète*, 1:193, 6:169, and 6:170, by permission of Artemis Verlag, Zurich.

Figures 47, 48, 50, and 51 were generously contributed by the National Museum of Western Art, Tokyo.

Figures 49 and 52 are reprinted from *Japan Architect* 34 (August 1959), by permission of The Japan Architect.

Figures 53–58 were generously contributed by the Huntington Museum of Art, Huntington, West Virginia (figure 58: photograph by Louis Reens).

Figures 59–64 are reprinted by permission of the Nationalgalerie, Berlin (figure 59: photograph by Jörg P. Anders; figures 60–64: photographs by Reinhard Friedrich).

Figure 65 was obtained from the Museum of Modern Art, New York.

Figures 66, 68, and 70–72 are reprinted by permission of the Museum of Modern Art, New York (figures 66, 70–72: photographs by Robert M. Damora).

Figures 67 and 69 are reprinted from *Architectural Forum* 71, no. 2 (February 1938): 116, 120.

Figure 73 is reprinted from *Werk* 66 (January 1979): 33, by permission of Werk, Bauen + Wohnen, Zurich.

Figures 74–79 are reprinted by permission of the National Gallery of Art, Washington, D.C.

Figures 80 and 91 are reprinted from *Domus* no. 566 (January 1977): 9, 11 by permission of Domus; Figure 91 also by permission of Renzo Piano and Richard Rogers.

Figures 81–83 are reprinted from *Domus* no. 503 (October 1971): 3, 5, 4, by permission of Domus; figures 82 and 83 also by permission of Renzo Piano and Richard Rogers.

Figure 84 was generously contributed by Neil Levine.

Figures 85 and 89 appeared in the book *Le Centre Georges Pompidou: Anatomie d'un batiment* (Paris: Editions du Centre Pompidou, 1977), and are reprinted by permission of the Centre Georges Pompidou (figure 85: photograph by Bernard Vincent).

Figures 86–88, 90, and 92 are reprinted from *Architectural Review* 161 (May 1977): 276, 294, 281, 282, and 280, by permission of The Architectural Press Ltd., London; figures 90 and 92 also by permission of Renzo Piano and Richard Rogers. (Figure 88: photograph by Martin Charles.)

Figures 93, 95, and 96 are reprinted by permission of the Centre Georges Pompidou, Paris (figure 93: photograph by D. Gliksman).

Figure 94 is reprinted from *Architectural Design* 47, no. 2 (1977): 122, by permission of Academy Editions, London.

Figures 97–99 and 101–106 were generously contributed by the Harvard University Art Museums, Cambridge, Massachusetts.

Figure 100 was generously contributed by James Stirling (photograph by John Donat).

Figures 107–109 were generously contributed by Timothy Hursley.

Index